The A Sacred Writing

Exploration–based Approaches to Transform and Heal Your Emotions, Beliefs and Experiences

A Collaboration

RITZ
BOOKS

The Art of Sacred Writing: Exploration-based Approaches to Transform and Heal Your Emotions, Beliefs and Experiences

Healing is a process, not a destination.

~Steph Ritz

Imagine you take a quantum leap
and land safely into your dream life.

~Michelle Bee, Searching for SHE

Table of Contents

Meet the Authors

The Art of Sacred Writing has two distinct parts: the writing exercises are designed by a certified educator (Steph Ritz) and a licensed therapist (Michelle Bee), and the narrative stories and poems illustrate our amazing power to transform - aligning who you are with what you believe.

Steph Ritz is the publisher and curator of this book series, and she's known for turning what you're saying into what you meant to say. When Steph's parents passed away 2 years apart, suddenly Steph was the only person left living that knew the stories behind world-famous paintings. Together with the publisher, Steph redesigned her stepdad's autobiography into a stunning coffee table art book and online sales system that stood strong for over a decade.

After fulfilling her parents' dying wish, Steph continued with a career in books, websites, and graphic design. Fifteen years later, Steph is an 11x international bestselling author, award-winning educator, and world renowned for her ghostwriting, photography, and publishing. Her imprint Ritz Books promotes giving back, advocating for, and raising awareness around diversity, sustainability, and social change. Steph creates sacred space to write from a meaningful and transformational perspective.

For the first time ever, Steph is sharing her signature process to reveal yourself through storytelling. She also shares an excerpt from her upcoming memoir, a chapter about the year she stepping to all the hobbies that would one day turn into a career.

Michelle Bee was in the 200-person audience the first time Steph shared a healing story from the stage. Moved to tears, she and Steph chatted, hugged it out, and became instant friends.

Around the same time, Michelle was scrolling through insurance billing codes, when she flipped to a page that had things like drama therapy, poetry therapy, art therapy - billable codes for expressive art therapy – and she immediately started researching poetry therapy. She found the National Association of Poetry Therapy, and instantly became a member. Then as fate would have it, she was able to attend the first ever Los Angeles expressive art therapy conference where she met tons of great mentors, received specialized training, and was invited to return two years later to facilitate a workshop as an Expressive Arts Therapist Trainee.

Seeing how in such a short session so much transformation happened with the expressive arts, Michelle was no longer interested in talk therapy. She wanted creative things that could touch people's hearts quickly, things that could help them feel seen and witnessed at the deepest levels, and sometimes words are not enough. Now, she is in the final stages of her training program to be a Certified Poetry Therapist.

When Steph offered a 30-day writing challenge (as seen in this book) Michelle created all the copywriting needed to build her website. A few years later, Michelle facilitated a 33-day journaling challenge that awakened the desire for Steph to start publishing. Yes, Michelle's therapeutic processes are that transformative! Here, Michelle shares a way for us to heal through poetry and journaling.

Radcliffe Johnson and Steph met at an event where they broke arrows with their throat, bent metal with their chest, and walked barefoot over broken glass and fire. He has curated a collection of poems that are honest and raw with emotional exploration.

Hasti Fashandi and Steph met in childhood, and though Hasti didn't know it at the time, her house was a safe place away from the terrors you'll read about in Steph's story. Here, Hasti shares tales of travesty and togetherness.

Kimberly "Omiseun" Early and Steph must have known each other in another lifetime, for the instant they met Steph ran up to Kimberly in recognition. Each time Kimberly reveals a part of herself, to Steph it feels like a remembering instead of a learning. They both advocated for teachers to be more mindful of their words and heal their own wounds.

Tomas El Rayess captivated Steph's tastebuds when he was cheffing for their mutual client during a deep dive sales page rewrite. Steph invited Tomas to cook soul-supportive food and facilitate sacred ceremony at her redwoods writing retreats. Tomas shows how one person's commitment to change can create healing ripples throughout many generations.

Introduction
Writing as Sacred Medicine

Rarely, if ever, are any of us healed in isolation.
Healing is an act of communion.

~ Bell Hooks, All About Love

This collaboratively written book is motivated by exploration-based approaches to see how your mindset and beliefs influence the way you get in touch with the wisdom and insights that come through you.

Do you feel a deep calling to breathe support and energy into your healing journey? Explore the sacred links between mind, mood, body, and beliefs – so you can see the potential that lies within your heart, uncover possibilities within yourself, and embrace soul-awakening healing.

There is a tremendous amount of research on prescriptive writing. Not only does it allow you to reframe memories, but it also improves your mindfulness, builds resiliency, and increases social and emotional intelligence. Committing to a therapeutic writing practice for 15 minutes a day, on a topic that you are emotionally invested in and feel is important, is all it takes to form a healing habit and build neuropathways.

Bibliotherapy, poetry therapy, journal writing, and storytelling are important healing tools that have the potential to reshape our understanding of how quickly we can heal. The goal of this book is to create a safe space for you to explore the links between mind, mood, body, and beliefs – so you can see the potential that lies within your heart, uncover possibilities within yourself, and embrace soul-awakening healing.

The majority of this book is based on a simple principle: when you shift, everything changes.

This book has been written to help you to come home to yourself.

It's so important to be in integrity with the unique expression of who you are – we want you to live a more aligned life, amplify your voice, and wake up with more joy.

Are you willing to let creativity and inspiration take the lead? Do you feel a deep calling to breathe support and energy into your healing journey? The Art of Sacred Writing was designed to help you dream with your eyes open, and to empower you with perception beyond sight. How committed are you to finding success through learning, growth, and healing?

You can intentionally design, develop, and implement your dreams to see them come true. But to get there, it'll take deep intentionality and time to examine your life and the ways in which you are ready to speak your inner truth.

By exploring holistic approaches to your healing journey, you can:

- Embrace and accept what comes in each moment.
- Allow in what you've been resisting.
- Find gratitude for your journey.
- Move forward with intention.

You can choose embodied ownership, where each experience shows how resilient you are – despite your circumstances – and leads you closer to becoming centered in the core of yourself.

Truly, you are strong enough to burst through any limiting belief that lurks within your thoughts.

With love,
Steph and Michelle

Finding Your Voice:
Position Your Expertise in Your Writing
Steph Ritz

As a ghostwriter who had written multiple books, I couldn't figure out how to share examples of my work without giving away the clients - I felt at a loss when I transitioned online. So back in 2015, I decided to rewrite my entire website with positioning stories – the magic I offer as a ghostwriter).

I created a question-based list of ideas I'd want new clients to communicate before beginning,

I created a question-based 3-part video series for when a new client would sign up for ghostwriting retreat or a copywriting deep dive called *The Welcome Gift*.

A couple years later in 2017, I turned the questions into *The 30-Day Writing Challenge*. Every day for a month, I filmed an unscripted video.

The words below are a combination of those video transcripts and the comments I left for the 267 participants who wrote with me during this 30-day challenge. Many people were able to write everything needed to build a website (including co-author Michelle) and many were also able to heal and called this sequence of questioning a cathartic process.

I built my business with Ritz Library! ~ Michelle Bee

For years both *Finding Your Voice* video courses were only available inside of *Ritz Library*, a private online video library of all my courses, which has recently been retired.

I surprised myself with some of the truths spoken into existence because of this questioning series. Spirit gave voice to what needed to be heard. Now it's your turn to find your writing voice.

Enjoy!

Steph Ritz is the publisher, graphic designer, coach and editor of this book. With dozens of international bestselling books, she is a world-renowned writer, web designer, and photographer. Steph combines cutting-edge writing techniques, deep connection, and taking effective action to create stories that change the world.

Hybrid Publishing with Ritz Books under the imprint "Ritz Books" yet managed from your Amazon account, so you get 100% of the royalties. Collaboration books donate their royalties to non-profits and scholarship funds. Both hybrid publishing and collaborative books include ghostwriting, editing, cover design, and layout.

If you want to connect more deeply with your vision and express your unique voice, Steph Ritz masterfully guides you through a process where you gain clarity and move into inspired action in one swoop. She does this with structured knowledge of branding, platform building, and a playful spirit. She will ask you to work the process until you have powerful words and images that mirror your authentic voice.
~ Michelle Bee, LMFT

The Welcome Gift (2015)

This 3-part puzzle reveals my #1 quick start tip on how to position yourself as an expert in your writing. Each of the 3 puzzle pieces reveal your life's stories in ways you might not have voiced them previously. When doing these idea shaping puzzles myself, I've seen things I never dreamed existed within me. And my writing has grown both professionally and personally because of dedicating time to examining and developing my own voice. These puzzle pieces are for you to meditate on, brainstorm around, and use as writing prompts.

Part 1: Shape Your Ideas

The typical journey of an entrepreneur is one where you work hard doing something you love with people you love. And when you take a break, lose confidence, or don't follow your passion and purpose, your true gifts pool up behind you like you've put a cork in a waterfall until...

Until the pressure is too much to contain the current and you go flying off the edge and find yourself clinging to the waterfall's ledge - grasping onto what was, and terrified to drop into the unknown watery depths below.

Just like the waterfall, your ideas are meant to flow into the hands of others.

What's little in your eyes may be awe inspiring to someone else. If you don't brag (the truth) who will? When you really look at how you can make a difference, opportunities will magically appear.

People are paying for the experience YOU provide. Share your successes, losses, and lessons learned with transparent honesty. You have to show the real you. If you don't, no one ever will understand your unique perspective. No one has your background. No one can bring your unique personality to the table.

Stop corking your waterfall of ideas and let it flow my friend! Trust where you're heading and dive deep into the wealth of what you have to offer. Follow the current of your unique purpose. Take some time to ask yourself questions until you get to the heart of your passions.

- Who were you when you were your own hero?
- When did you rescue yourself?
- Who were you before the world told you who to be?
- Who were you three, five, and 10 years ago?

Consider your hero stories, examine the puzzle pieces that make you uniquely and authentically you.

Part 2: Organize Your Actions

Getting your message across begins by communicating clearly developed ideas. Your ideas are the heart of your message – and your voice is how you share your heart with the world. Have you ever said, "Who me?" when someone shared that your words inspired them?

A recent client said to me, "I felt naked, like you could see right through me. You saw everything I thought I was hiding from the world - you took my heart and turned it into words."

Who, me? Well, when I look from her perspective I can totally see why she described our work in such endearing terms. One of the biggest struggles when talking about yourself is getting comfortable using terms that accurately describe what you've done and what you're doing in a way that makes sense to your community.

How you share your hero story should enrich and develop your main idea. It's important to start small and, when the small things start adding up, consider how they led you forward on the gigantic steps you've taken.

With a specific idea in mind, you can be clear and concise while sharing a deeper understanding of your passionate journey to where you are today. Often your journey parallels what your ideal clients have been walking.

1. Who is your community/tribe/audience?
2. What do they already know?
3. What do you want them to know?
4. Do you share enough details to convey you know their needs?

5. What details can you add to be able to meet their expectations?
6. Why is your idea interesting?
7. Why is your message important?
8. Do your words communicate your passion?
9. Is your idea easy to understand?

Sit with these 9 questions and see what shape your puzzle begins to take.

Part 3: Voice Your Passions

There are many ways to bring an idea to life within real-life situations. There are obvious ways to make an impression and there are subtle ways to show depth. Stories serve as a way to ground your ideas – they help your reader connect your message to their prior knowledge.

Share your emotions to breathe life into your message. In every culture, emotions are the same. Love, hate, frustration, compassion... they're all universal emotions. Let us feel what you felt, let us experience what you experienced, let us yearn to grow - just as you have done.

Who we are and what we've experienced influences how we learn. No one sees quite what you see when you're sharing your expertise. What does the reader need to know without previously having heard of you? What do they need in order to understand your unique perspective?

So what is it about the way you share your experiences that draws people into your story?

Knowing how to find your voice is essential to being a successful writer. No matter what you're writing, you have bits of your personality that seep into your writing and those bits strengthen the unique perspective you bring when you voice your passions.

- When did you listen, learn, and grow?
- How did you make someone's life a bit better?
- Why did you move forward?
- Did you move forward realistically and positively?
- What did you appreciate in the journey?

Listen for the rhythms of your unique perspective that arise naturally when your ideas flow in alignment with your passions.

So the #1 quick start tip? Find your voice. It's a sure way to position yourself as an expert in your writing.

That's all for now. Good luck sorting through your puzzle pieces. I look forward to working with you soon!

30 Day Writing Challenge (2017)

Each day I'm going to share a question that hopefully will let you break into showing us your story instead of you telling us a story.

What is a Positioning Story?

Instead of telling me you earned xyz degree, tell me a story of an experience that influenced you during that time so I can see how you came to be the awesomeness that's you. These are your stories of moving away from victimhood and co-dependency. This process is for you to figure out how to take everything that you've experienced and turn it into words that the readers, us, can experience just as you experienced it by the way that you share your story.

It's about translating your experiences into offers, whether that's time with you or a product that you have. Maybe you're trying to pitch yourself for a job. You never know.

What I do know is that the minute that you start telling someone who you are, they tune out. We are all looking at life through our own lens. We've all had experiences. If you can break into the listener's experience with the way that you share your words, now that is writing that converts. That's what we're focusing on here.

Each day, I'll ask you a question. I'll share a couple of ideas of how that might look for you. Then I'll share a little bit of what that looked like for me in the past.

What are you writing into existence?

These are your stories and you're the only person who knows the world from your eyes. The goal is to create an experience with your words. We're here to build each other up. My core beliefs include mutual respect, honesty, and caring... so this is what I will mirror and ask my tribe to reflect.

Yes, always stay true to your heart!

Have you ever listened to your body while you're retelling an experience? Isn't it fascinating that our bodies know there's something amiss before we find out what's wrong?

These are deep and vulnerable shares. It takes a community to create the change: first awareness, then the shift can begin.

Yes, we're here to bring each other up collectively.

Has your body ever broken out with goosebumps at the thought, "This is bigger than me,"? This is a call to step into your dreams. And once your dreams are real, I can't wait to hear you say "Now what, what next?" as you keep dreaming bigger and following your heart message.

Have you given your gifts to yourself? This is something I learned late in life, and it changed everything.

Yes, these questions are huge. To be honest. I put myself through this writing challenge twice a year or more. The last thing I want is for this process to be scary. The trick is to answer with the story you feel most called to share.

When I sit down to write from a prompt, usually 3-4 story threads run through my head. Think of the biggest questions you get asked over and over AND OVER again until you're blue in the face. Who are you, what do you do, how long have you been doing it? Can you answer these questions with story illustrations instead of stating facts?

There are no wrong answers, only different tales to tell. How can you show us what you've experienced. I want to know how the uniform fits you, why writing on water bottles (affirmations and intentions) matter to you. I want to know what I don't know to ask you because I just haven't been a part of your life journey for that long.

I've been a horseback riding instructor, archery teacher, caregiver, photographer, chocolatier, fine art vendor, pre-school teacher, ghostwriter, coffee barista.... the list goes on. And each experience has a handful of experiences I could choose to share that I think would illustrate that time of my life. The important thing is that you choose any one story thread and start writing.

Day 1:

Who were you when you rescued yourself?

I know some of the times that I've seen people go into rescue mode that really shifted their life is after a trauma or while they're grieving after a death. It may have been times when they felt cornered and didn't know how to make a choice. There might have been times when you only had one path to walk, and you didn't like it.

For me one of those times is when I felt 100% cornered in my house and trapped. I lost my immune system. I couldn't walk around the block because I was too exhausted.

That meant that my entire business dried up. I was a ghostwriter getting on a plane every three months to go work with millionaires to take their ideas from creation into final product. When you don't have an immune system, you can't travel, right?

At that moment, when I felt I had no other options, that's the moment when I decided to go online. I built myself a website in one weekend. Yes, that was about 30 hours shoved into just one weekend where I studied all the videos and popped it out. I launched it, started a video series and landed clients.

Even though I felt totally cornered with no options, I was the person who stood up to rescue myself.

Please find yourself called to take action with your words - breathe with your ideas, smile because of the memories, and type through the tears.

Each step forward is a heroic moment. Vision is super important, but so is courage.

There's a lot of room for interpretation in the questions I'll be asking. Usually, I ask you to write whatever idea was triggered. For instance, the word "rescue" can be very triggering, but how did you find your way out of (or save someone from) a dangerous or distressing situation?

What stories can illustrate the trigger for a new path, an opportunity? Like when I realized in my last semester student teaching that I couldn't be in the classroom and on call as a caregiver for my grandma at the same time. So I rewrote a guy's website and sent the revised version to him saying I'd heard he was interested in writing a book. Less than a week later, I was in the giant California redwoods in his living room working on my 2nd book project. At the time, I felt between a rock and a hard place. Really, it was a door opening into a new future.

Day 2:
When did you become your own hero?

I remember waking up at 18 years old to my grandma falling against my door. She was having a major stroke.

We were in the middle of the countryside an hour away from the hospital. I had no clue what to do. She couldn't feel half of her body. Yet I somehow managed to still get her up and drive in the snow for the first time with no incident, even though a couple feet of snow had already fallen overnight.

I got her to the hospital in time for her to keep most of her cognitive abilities. Yes, she lost her short-term memory, but she kept all the old ones. That meant that she was able to live alone with massive assistance.

Being her hero was a moment when I also became my own hero, because I also became her caregiver. Had I not acted so swiftly, I wouldn't have been able to be there for her because she wouldn't have been able to be in her own home.

I managed to have 11 years with the matriarch of our family, caring for her and her caring for me. I wouldn't trade anything in the world to have gone a different path in life. That makes me so happy and strong because I knew, in that moment, I stood up and did something that I didn't think I could do. I did it anyway.

Now I look back and I really realize how it brought me to where I am. For years I was my grandma's voice, and she was my song. Without that song, I still don't know what I'd be singing today.

So when is it that you became your own hero? What happened? What lit you up? What were you doing when you realized you were about to put on the Batman cape and take off into the sky?

Day 3:
Who were you before the world told you who to be?

This is an intense question that I have sat with many times myself. Today, the first couple of answers that popped in my thoughts felt like they were more conditioned responses. They were stories that I told myself in the past. They might not be my stories, rather a story that was told to me.

I took this question today into morning meditation. What came forward for me were different images of myself throughout the ages of my life, always sitting at water's edge in forested areas. I grew up living on a river with a big back yard and all sorts of trees. I had my favorite thinking rock that I would go sit on.

My grandma lived on a lake. We'd go and spend summers there. Often, I'd just sit on the water's edge listening to the waves from wind lap against the rocks. This continued all the way forward into the writing retreats that I run. They are surrounded by redwoods on a lakefront with streams running all over the property.

I went deep within and found the answer that really says why I'm doing what I'm doing now. I don't know if I really saw that full connection previously. Of course I've always loved being in nature, but did I realize that that was my happy place throughout my life? I'm not sure.

All I've ever wanted was to be grounded in nature where I could listen to the water's rhythm...

Now as a spiritual adult, I can see how my Capricorn sun and Pisces moon might have drawn me to these situations. It's no surprise I offer writing retreats in the giant California redwoods next to lakes and rivers - spots tucked in the trees and connected to Native American land.

After my mom died, I left school with only 3 classes left in my degree and headed to New Jersey to deal with the estate and art business. In that year away, I separated my parents' stuff from the art business stuff. Every day, I'd walk to the end of the block to listen to the river - trying to figure out if tide was coming in or going out. We were so close to the ocean; the pushback swelled the river in tune to the rising tide. As a Midwesterner, I was fascinated. I was grateful for the bench under a big shade tree to sit in silence. We all heal in different ways, and this ritual soothed my grieving soul. Over 2 years, I'd said an eternal goodbye to them both...

My stepdad lived in that house for over 50 years - he'd added a 2-story artist's studio to the back end and stood for hours at the easel even into his last week of life at the age of 89. I loved how he'd sit in his chair reading and try to "catch" the painting from a new perspective to see what strokes to make next and which brush would bring it alive.

The art was spread everywhere in the house... open a book and a sketch falls out, go through the old taxes and find letters between Stanley and Norman Rockwell about the 1976 national phonebook cover, go through the garage and find new paintings! It was a mess. My mom had started the sorting process, but her cancer had come back and the aggressive radiation and chemo treatments were draining and time consuming.

We spent an hour a day for my first week as her terminal caregiver in the studio, her showing me the systems she had started and explaining all the moving parts of running the home-based fine-arts business she'd been captaining for the past 9 years. Over 3 months, I did what no one wants to do - I watched my mom lose her life to a freckle on her toe.

And from the chaos came creation: I'd fulfilled my stepdad and mom's dying wishes of getting my stepdad's autobiography + biography published. My siblings and I sold the business to the publisher, who had now had a beautiful coffee table book that perfectly positioned nearly every painting remaining in the estate. And so a career in positioning was born.

A year later, when I went back to school, my last professor in my undergrad Education / Language Art degree was a professor from the Oneida reservation. As a bonus, she invited us out to their learning center for an end of term powwow. This was my normal... I was thrilled to be back in the trees with the ancestors of the land. The last certification I got back in Wisconsin before moving to California was called "TRIBES Learning Communities". Looking at the ways of our ancestors and to the future of our great-grandchildren - the true meaning of sustainability.

My soul craved healing.

What is it that you believe? What are the negatives you've absorbed and are choosing to change, therefore claiming their untruth?

What are the unseen forces guiding us?

Who were you before the world told you who to be?

Day 4:
Who were you three years ago?

Today's question is to take a journey back into your own life, but really look at it from what your story is telling your community. What are they learning? What are they going to be able to shortcut from their experience because you've already experienced it, learned from it and are bringing that knowledge forward?

Who were you three years ago? Not who you were last year, 20 years ago, but exactly three years ago? The question is asked like this because typically, psychologically it takes three years to have enough distance to understand why things unfolded the way that they did and how it brought you to where you are now.

Three years ago, for me, I was working in social media. I was living in Wisconsin with a man who was abusive. He controlled me. He had even bruised a rib, yet I hadn't left him.

Three years ago, I had a wakeup call. I woke up to lying to myself, my friends and my family. No one knew what I was going through. I was living in my own silence and my own fear of what I had actually gone through.

How could I, such a strong powerful woman, end up in an abusive relationship and still be there? That's not cool, right? What I realized is that my business could only ever grow as healthy as the other aspects of my life.

With my relationship in ruins, it wasn't happening. My business was really stuck. I just didn't know how to go forward. In releasing him, I created space to move my health, self-care and business forward in gigantic ways that really supported me, who I am and the gifts that I can bring to you.

Who were you three years ago?

Yes, the Universe really does conspire to bring you all you desire when you are super clear about what you want. Take a stand for yourself in any situation, and used the tools available to you as you hold space for your intentions. The more you move through fear and into the unknown, the more that fear will try to pull you back.

Healing thru process is magnificent! When I feel the change deep within, I know something big is happening – that it's already in motion even though I have no clue which dots will connect to what... beautiful.

Day 5:
Who were you five years ago?

I've heard it said that, when you share your story, you're actually sharing the memory of the last time that you told that story. That's a huge reason why I put myself through these exercises at least once a year, if not twice a year. The questions change as you change. The years change as you change.

When I look at this question, for me I find this one very difficult to answer. It's not because I can't remember. It's because of what was going on in my life.

About this time exactly five years ago, my grandma had just passed away about a week or so prior. She is someone that had been a part of my life always, as well as I a part of hers, being her caregiver for 11 years after her strokes.

All of that was gone. Think empty nest times 1,000, right? At the same time, the family came for the end of life, ransacked the house, packed what they wanted, took the pictures off of the walls and left.

I was sitting in my grandma's house, a total mess from everyone coming through. I thought that I had poison ivy. My sister had gotten some poison ivy on her ankles. We're in Wisconsin in the

woods on a lake. It was so typical to get poison ivy out there...
even though I'd never gotten it.

It got worse and worse. I started throwing up. I started waking up
in the middle of the night sick. I couldn't figure out what was going
on. I went to a walk-in clinic around the block from my house.

I had bought a house within two blocks of the largest major
hospital in the area, which is where we saw grandma's end of life.

Everyone came. I had 13 people staying at my house. We all
helped her cross over to the next life together through hospice in
the hospital.

I had nothing. I was sick and miserable. I walked into this clinic
telling the guy that saw me, this old man, about how I think I have
poison ivy, and I'm at the cottage.

I show it to him. He says, "Oh, well do you have it anywhere else?"
It was next to my bellybutton on my side right above my hip. I
point out a spot on the back side. They were mirror images front
and back. He says, "Oh, you have shingles." I said, "Wait. What?
That old people disease?" He said, "Yeah, you have shingles."

Then I remembered that someone else on the ICU level of the
hospital had shingles. I must have picked it up from them. That
didn't explain waking up sick, not being able to eat and throwing
up all the time. None of that was explained. It really didn't feel like
grief.

As we start talking, what the doctor tells me is that I probably or
most likely have something called C. diff. It's one of those hospital
super bugs that knocks out your immune system. It kills off all of
the healthy gut bacteria and grows its own instead.

What he told me were two very specific things that changed
everything in the way that I would get cared for in the next year or
so. The first was that I wasn't supposed to be able to get the
disease.

C. diff was only open to people that were on antibiotics. I wasn't,
but my grandma had been on huge amounts of drip IV antibiotics.
I had spent a lot of time holding her hand, rubbing her arms and
touching her to let her know that I was there for her. I had
absorbed enough of her antibiotics to open my system up.

I sat in the doctor's office. He told me that no one was going to believe that I had C. diff. and that it was really hard to get a positive answer that it was C. diff. He said that if I didn't fight for myself, then I would never get healthy again. The situation that I got sick in was so improbable and so unrealistic that I was the only person who was going to stand for myself.

It took another two or three months before I got the diagnosis that it actually was C. diff. It took a year plus before anyone even told me what probiotics were. I'd never known. Natural medicine is what brought me back to where I am today. It's amazing work.

Do I want to share this story? No. Is what I'm sharing now different than the last time that I told this story two years ago? Abso-freakin-lutely.

Who were you five years ago? Can you share that person with us, and what you were struggling with and going through in your life?

It's amazing work that you're doing.

These stories are so beneficial, and bring you forward. It might sound like we're going through a cathartic experience, or we're just sharing our experiences to share. The reality is that we connect to others on mutual understanding and mutual respect.

By sharing little snippets of my life, you're able to see and understand where I've been. That doesn't mean that you have to have been in the same place, but that you can connect to something that I said. It might be a time when you were so sick or a time when no one believed what you were saying.

What is it that you connected with in my story that allows you to resonate with the words that I said and to listen and be engaged? That's something for you to consider as you write your stories.

My dreams have always guided me, and I listen to them because I trust my deep inner voice to take control of the scene it's creating in my mind when I let go of control. I feel I've been walking between two worlds, sometimes bumping shoulders in a brick walled alley and other times stumbling sideways and slipping behind the veil only to be jolted back out again into the in between. Truth is only as true as the moment it lives within. And every day I question what is true today.

Day 6:
Who were you 10 years ago?

I know some of us have more than 10 years to go back, but we're creating a line of thought. It's where you were 10 years ago that brought you to where you were 5 years ago that brought you to where you were 3 years ago. We're just currently working backwards.

You can do 10 years, and then you can keep playing with this exercise. Can you go back 20 or 50 years? How many decades do you have to play with? Keep telling stories and show how every single step you took brought you to where you are today.

For me, 10 years ago I had already received a writing degree. I was a caregiver for my grandma where I'd visit her a couple times a week to take care of her. I was a full-time straight A student. I also worked full time at a video store. Life was quite interesting back then.

Exactly 10 years ago, I was running a local chapter at my college for a national organization. Now, just to give you a heads up, I'm going to get a bit political...

My grandpa was sterile. My grandma participated in some of the first artificial inseminations out there. For me, having the right to choose has nothing to do with abortion. It is about choosing what's right for you. I wouldn't exist had that option not been available to my grandma. It was very controversial at the time.

With that note, I want to give you a heads up that, exactly 10 years ago, I was running a pro-choice chapter on my campus. What we really focused on and worked on as a network across the state and the nation was to get the Morning After Pill, which is birth control, over the counter for women.

At the time, you needed a prescription. Even when you'd go to the hospital, no one was required to tell you that there was a pill you could take. It's not about getting pregnant or about making an abortion. It's about changing your hormones so that your period comes early.

I know personally one of the things that I always came back to was that if I were raped, I'd want to know that there was an option. It wasn't required to tell anyone. It was not widely known at the time. It was not over the counter.

You had to go to a hospital where they may, or may not, write you a prescription. At the time, anything that was a religious affiliated hospital would refuse to give prescriptions. It was ridiculous. It's birth control. At least that's how I felt.

Knowing that and looking at my entire life, I've always been an advocate for what I felt was right and for the right of choice. It's the same thing today that you get to choose what you do with your life. Whatever it is that you're doing, you get to choose.

Your life is designed based on the choices that you have made and the choices that you are getting ready to make. You know what? That's a pretty beautiful thing.

You never have any clue what you're setting in motion with the choices you make... Even though you don't realize it at the time, it always turns out to be exactly what you need for a massive shift to happen.

Day 7:
Who is your community?

Today, just like the past couple of days, we're starting a new multi-thread story. Today we are starting a three piece. I want to explain it all so that you know how to look at it separately as well as where we're going.

Over the next couple of days, we're going to be looking at who's your community, your tribe and your audience? These are three separate questions. Typically, the way I look at it is that your audience is the general population of anyone that might happen to come across who you are and listen for two seconds.

They may cross your Facebook, or stumble on a webpage. They're the general population. They're cold. You've never heard of them. They've never heard of you.

The community are people who've heard of you, but they might not have worked with you. They might have as well. The community tends to be people who are already familiar with who you are. They have self-selected into hanging out with you, your genius and what you're offering within your business.

Your tribe is the inner circle. The people who really understand what it is that you offer, and how truly beneficial it is to them to choose you and your services as the solution that they really need.

Today we're only looking at one of those three pieces. Where we are going to start is your community. Whether you share who your community is in relation to audience or to tribe, or you give a standalone example doesn't matter. What matters is that you differentiate between the three different types of people who come your way.

Here is an example of my community. When I look back a few years ago after I got really sick and didn't have an immune system, I didn't know how to continue with my business. I transitioned everything online. In order to do that, I reached out to friend who is a virtual assistant. She started outsourcing a couple of tasks here and there to me.

There's no way that I could take on another book project. I didn't trust my own self not to end up in the hospital next week, you know? How could I possibly feel like I could commit to someone when I couldn't commit to myself?

She started outsourcing projects to me. Slowly but surely, creep, creep, creep, a few hours turned into over 40 hours a week. It was at a price point that was way below what I had been earning prior to getting sick and transitioning online.

It wasn't okay with me. Yet I let it happen because there were some major things going on. I was learning from her community as well as building my own online community for the first time.

She understood. She could have been my tribe. That whole group was really right on the nose of what I was doing. I just wasn't able to talk about it, and I wasn't trusting myself.

They had me writing sales pages and website copy and doing voice branding and social media. Meanwhile, I learned all sorts of skills of how to market myself online and how to do it strategically with my own voice and with words.

I'm a content creator. That's what I do. I create words that express who you are so that other people can find you. Whether that's your speech or your talk, they had me building and editing ebooks.

Everything that I did when I was outsourcing myself to a virtual assistant, everything, was completely inside of my genius zone. It was me who had left my own tribe and stepped into the community role where I didn't believe who I was.

I didn't have self-confidence in the work that I was doing. It was partially because I was being told that this is what I was worth. It took a long time for me to be able to stand up for myself and to change that role.

Who are you? Who is your community? Who's your tribe? Who's your audience? Today I ask you to focus on just, who is your community, and share with us.

My community is filled with visionary experts - people who know they have a gift for the world, a vision of changing lives. My community is bettering everyone around them, detached from competitive and scarcity mindsets. They see their experiences as life's lessons and know they are a lifelong learner. They challenge themselves and stretch their comfort zone edge. They both get and give support to their inner circle. And they're in the game of turning dreams to reality.

Day 8:
Who's in your tribe?

Yesterday we were looking at who's really in your community. That's different from your audience and your tribe. Today we are looking at the types of people that are in your tribe.

When I say, "Who's in your tribe?" I don't mean what age are they? What profession are they? Where do they live? What do they do?

I mean, what are the core foundational philosophies of life that you and they share? How will they be able to trust your guidance will be in alignment with who they are and what they believe?

For me, I know that my tribe is full of heart-based professionals. They're different than my community that is full of visionary experts. Everyone in my tribe is also a visionary expert, but they are being guided through this world by giving of their heart and their message. They're not doing this to track down a paycheck.

It's a very different mentality if money is your biggest driver in life. My biggest driver is giving of myself freely so that those who are healers can help the people who need it the most. It's so that they can hear the call to come get the healing.

For me, I know that every one of my tribe has committed to consciously creating their future and their moment of every single day as well as where they're going. For that reason, they've come here. They know that they need to change how they're communicating to really turn their conscious creation in conscious communication as well.

That is my tribe.

Who's in your tribe? How can they recognize and trust who you are?

Though my tribe and I share many things, being heart-centered is something we all have in common. That doesn't mean being a starving artist, money is a benefit of sharing my heart message and gifts with the world. My tribe understands that words can change the world and they've committed themselves to consciously creating. My tribe is motivated by a deep desire to heal their communication so their community can hear the call from the audience and be able to self-select into walking from audience to community and then into the tribe if they're a fit. Picking up what I'm laying down?

I choose to use the word tribe in full respect to the word, the lineage of the people and to natives of all lands. One of my certifications as an educator is in building Tribes Learning Communities.

Tribe to some is a stereotype - yet as an educator, I feel it is extremely important to bring awareness and acceptance to the deeper connection of the word.

I spent many hours studying with Native Americans in Wisconsin, discussing exactly this, especially referencing educating others and the appropriateness of language.

The last thing I want is to be disrespectful to Native Americans, and all other tribes of our world.

Rather the opposite – my desire is to break any negative stereotypes associated with the word tribe and to bring forward the deep richness of the cultures of the world. It is good to question beliefs and motivations behind the choice to use certain words. Claiming the word "tribe" as American is inherently incorrect and half the problem of keeping the stereotype alive.

Bring your awareness to a deeper understanding. We are obligated to go beyond tolerance, even beyond acceptance, and truly embrace understanding each other.

Here's how a friend describes it:

" Tribe by definition is: "a group of people United by common descent and sharing common customs". As a Native American I do not take offense to your usage of the term, Steph. You apply it as defined and leave no hint of negative implication. My Anishnabe tribe is Potawatomi. As a family, my daughters and significant other are my tribe. As writers, women, entrepreneurs and lovers of this earth, YOU are my tribe. "Tribe" is a term introduced and defined by a "tribe" of non-native people and is commonly used to distinguish various "groups" of Native Americans. Any word can be used and implied with negative connotation but I myself have never been offended with the way you speak of your tribe. I find it to be a beautiful connection. I myself am more irritated with the use of the term "Indian"

~ Kelly Tovar

The word tribe originated to describe a group of people. I invite us all into a more global understanding of the word.

Day 9:
Who are you talking to in the audience?

We've looked at our tribe and our community. Today we're talking about the general population, our audience. There are four things that I always keep in mind when I'm looking at audience:

The 4 A's:

1. What are they *Assuming*?
2. What are they *Agreeing*?
3. What are they going to *Argue*?
4. What do they *Aspire* to do?

On that same front, what am I *assuming*? What am I making *agreements* on that I'm asking them to agree with me? What am I going to *argue* in their current beliefs? What am I *aspiring* to do for them, for myself and for the world? Just keep it in *The 4 A's* and you should be good.

An example of this is that tomorrow I'm going to be a guest teacher for a publisher. I'm coming in to teach a little class called Write Your Book Right. I am assuming that everyone who is there, coming from this publisher's audience, are all writing a book. I'm assuming that they all want to do it right.

They might be coming across some limiting beliefs. They might be wrapped up in analysis paralysis. I'm going to give them some concepts to argue with themselves to switch their thinking. In that same time, I want to aspire to inspire them. Pretty simple, right?

No matter who you're talking to, if you keep *The 4 A's* in mind, you'll very comfortably and easily talk to your community.

I know one thing that people come to me arguing. They say, "Well, you're a hard salesman, right?" No, I'm a heart salesman. We are not slimy marketing people. We are not using tricks and slime and gross. We're talking from our heart. For those who agree, they get to choose to walk with us forward.

Who are you talking to when you're talking to an audience? How can you use *The 4 A's* to move them into your community or tribe?

Any *assumptions*, *agreements*, *aspirations*, or *arguments* pop out from the words I've shared? I would LOVE to see you write a love letter to yourself about non-negotiable agreements of care for self that mirrors the same depth of care you offer others. How can you let your strength seep into your words?

Day 10:
What do they already know?

Over the last few days, we've been really considering who it is that we're talking to. Who's in the audience? Who's in the community? Who's in your tribe?

When we started looking at the four As yesterday, we're going to start carrying that forward more into what's inside of these people already.

Today we're looking at, what do they already know? When I say "they" you can choose one, or you can choose all at the same time. It's really up to you and what you're developing.

I know when I'm writing for myself or writing for clients, and we're writing a script or a talk, that we tend to really look at who is in the audience that we think would be a good fit for our community. If I'm writing website copy, then I'm very specifically speaking to people in my tribe.

One person at a time who is sitting on the other side of the screen, reading the words as if it were a letter to them.

When I'm writing, there are some assumptions that can be made especially when you're talking to your tribe. You've already assumed that they are in the right place, the right community and with the right people.

When I look at you or look at my tribe, there are some things that I think you already know. You tend to have more natural knowledge than I do. I grew up in a house where everyone could identify not only the plant name, but the plant species and everything about it. Yes, I have some of that knowledge, but nowhere near the depth of understanding that my mom or siblings have of the natural world.

One of the other things that people, myself included and my tribe, realize that you have to invest in yourself. Whether that be in the form of self-care or getting the education you need to get your message out there, you need to consistently invest in yourself.

With an empty cup there's nothing left to pour for others. You have to keep refilling your own. With what spills over the edge of your abundance is what you give to other people.

At the same time, I know that I'm a giver. I've learned the hard way that I really only get to work with givers from now on, no more takers. I know that my tribe understands what it's like to be a giver and to have had others take advantage of that. They want to find people who will give to them the same level that they give of themselves.

Some of those other little pieces are that you guys are all geniuses. You know what your gift is, and you know that you need to bring it forward so the people who need what you have and the healing that needs to take place in this world can happen.

Those are some things that I can assume about you. If I'm writing a page, or if I'm talking to my copy, I know that you guys know what's getting on. When I mention the different colors of green and spring on the trees where it's all yellowy and soft versus the green in autumn when the leaves are thick, lush, dark and vibrant with the heat of summer, you understand what I'm talking about. Could you probably put some more scientific words to it? Yes. That's okay.

What is it that your tribe, community and audience already know?

Show me YOUR heart of gold.
We all want a better world.
We are the dreamers.
We give (and give and give).
We know the change we want to see has to start with us.
I'm tired of generic.
Of people talking about problems.
And ignoring benefits.
And dismissing solutions.
I'm tired of flash that covers fluff.
Show me YOUR heart of gold.

Day 11:
What do you want them to know?

Yesterday we looked at what they already know so that we can start creating some assumptions and speaking directly to them instead of at them.

Today, what is it that you want them to know?

This changes based on what you're writing for and who you're writing to. Choose one of the three groups and speak to that person or someone in that audience, community or your tribe. Tell them what you want them to know.

Let's say I was speaking to someone in my book community or someone who is sitting on the edge and thinking, "I know I have these books inside of me, at least one if not three. I have to get it out, but writing just feels so hopeless. It's an endless amount of writing."

I would tell them that writing doesn't have to be difficult. It can be effortless. It can be efficient if you get the right support and surround yourself with a community that can bring you up, and it's all working towards the same thing. It's staying accountable together.

Let's say I was talking to someone who's writing their copy, then I would want them to know about whatever they're writing or what sits on the web page. If they can't read it out loud, then it's not their authentic voice. It's not going to resonate at the deepest level possible.

It's the same thing as writing a talk. I write and rewrite and rewrite and rewrite. Then, before going on stage, I set the script down and speak from my heart whatever comes forward. You can only prepare so much. You might as well take the time to do it right and to do it authentically. That's what I want you to know.

What is it that you want them to know?

Stand strong in your truth. Walk down the path of embodying the best version of your true self in words, feelings, actions, physical presence, and energetically. The cup is neither half full nor half empty - it's refillable.

I suggest capturing your scattered ideas in a list. I have a long list of stories to tell that haven't been given voice yet. The list of thought threads is like opening a treasure chest of gold spools when I sit down to weave my words.

Life's circumstances can either make you or break you. You can learn from every situation (even the crummy ones) and any issue you have ever been through in life. Give us something tangible we can grip.

Day 12:
Do you share enough details to convey you know their needs?

This gets a little complicated, but it's one of the biggest issues that I see in books, copy and general communication of people trying to explain themselves. I'll go to someone's website, and every single product on their site, every single offer, program and everything sounds like it was written for the exact same person – ANYONE.

Ask yourself, what is it that you need to share? What details will really convey that you know their needs?

When I looked at writing my sales page for the retreat, Write Your Book in Paradise, one of the things that I really looked at was acknowledging that these people are already experts.

I cannot make you an expert. However, I can show you how to take your own credibility and use that to position your own expertise, which is a very different discussion.

At the same time, I'm about to launch a course called Writing That Converts. That course is very specifically written. It's not just getting it out. It's not about just making you an expert.

It's about looking at the stories that align with you, align with your clients and align with the offer that you're giving or talking about. Even if the offer is to have a conversation. Maybe the offer is for them to stand up, get off of their couch, go outside and hug a tree.

Whatever it is, you have to share that you acknowledge the person that's on the other side, not the "anyone over there." What details can you share from your own life and your own experience and bring it into why you're offering what you offer?

Do you share enough details? If you don't, then what can you add to truly convey that you know what they need and what they want? Need can get a little tricky. I don't like to tell anyone what they need.

At the same time, we often with our self-talk tell ourselves what we need. We say, "I need a business coach. I need to get this launch off the ground. I need to call my grandma. I need to...I need to..."

We have very few basic human needs, but it's how we talk to ourselves. Pick your language. Convey your meaning. Ask yourself, "Do you share enough details to convey that you know their needs?"

What can you add to take your message from generic to one that generates engagement?

Day 13:
What details can you add to be able to meet their expectations?

This question is really about setting yourself and the person you're speaking to up for success. Knowing their expectations up front makes it easier for you to be able to slide into that as the finish line of where you wrap up.

One of the things that I very rarely mention, and always surprises my clients, is that I build websites. So far, about 99% of all of my web work has been done completely by me. It's not something that I advertise.

Yes, I can pop online. I can set you up with a basic WordPress website. I can get MailChimp up for you and get some JotForms going so that you can capture emails. I can set up a five-pager for you in a couple of hours.

At the same time, it's not my genius work. Though now I can read some coding, I'm not that good at going in. I can pick a theme that's responsive that you like and put it in. I can put a page builder in for you so it's really easy plug and play, but it's not a service that I offer.

What catches me though, is that last week I had someone come over. I gave her everything that I just described as part of a service of our working together. She said that she's paid someone $5,000 to set her up with a basic WordPress site. That's something that I did in two hours for free, pretty much, because she was already under contract.

Then it comes up again yesterday. Someone was saying, "I don't know what to do. I need all of this done." I said, "Really? Do you just want me to do this for you? I can make this happen."

Knowing how to build websites, how all of these different pieces work together and how to put them together so that they play nicely, really boosts my copywriting skills and my communication skills. Knowing how the words are laid out on the page is as important as the words on the page.

Both of those are reasons why I'm a copywriter who has gotten super strong results for over 10 years for copywriting clients. It's because I understand both the design of the words and the meaning that the words carry.

What details can you add to be able to meet their expectations? I have now set up the expectation that I understand the tech land or tech world and can help you there. Even though I'm not doing that, it makes sense why my words flow and why they've been so game changing for other people.

What skills, knowledge, or perspective can you share to help give them a clearer picture of what to expect?

Day 14:
Why is your idea interesting?

I'd like for you to answer this with a story in mind, not just telling us what's interesting about it.

Here's an example. Yesterday I went up to my upstairs neighbor's apartment. We started chatting. She's moving in about a week because L.A. hasn't been kind to her. She's gone from job to job to job selling. She's a massage therapist. She's had a really hard time finding work here. We started talking.

I've had the exact opposite reaction. I've lived in L.A. and moved here just a couple of days before the beginning of this year.

It hasn't even been a year. L.A. has been so welcoming to me. It's opened its arms as if to say, "Thank you for finally being here.

My business skyrocketed. Everything has been going lovely. I cannot complain because my life is more ideal than I ever could have imagined in my dreams. The difference is that since moving here I have dedicated my entire focus to giving myself the same gifts that I give my clients.

For years and years, I've been writing books and website copy, helping people position themselves online and really create a distinctive branded voice for their business. I'd never done the same for myself. This is my gift, and yet I'd never used it on myself.

Since moving here, I've been taking everything that I do, the methods, formulas, processes and sequences, and I've been using them on myself. Holy cow am I a hard teacher! I understand if it's been a little rough for you, but it's in the best interest of your growth and how you are voicing your passion so that others can hear that call.

Why is your idea interesting? Why is my idea interesting? It's because it's working. I'm the fable. I moved to L.A. and "made it." It was easy because I voiced my passions with stories. I gave myself what it is that I have to give. It shifted everything within me internally as well as how I'm showing up for my clients.

Why is your idea interesting? What story can you share to illustrate why it fascinates you and why your work fascinates others?

You HAVE to show the real you. Knowing it and living it are 2 different things. What we offer is often what we need the most. How have you benefited from your own gifts? Why do others geek out about you?

Day 15:
Why is your message important?

Congratulations on making it halfway. Fifteen days of writing is a lot more than most people do. It's easy to journal or to write a few notes. To really focus on the words that are going to move your business forward is a lot more dedication than most.

Even with YouTube videos, Zoom-type meetings and telephone calls, still the number one way that we communicate to the tune of multi-billion dollars a year is email. It's number one hands down.

If you're in business, then you're a writer whether or not you like it.

That brings us to today's question, which is, why is your message important? Why should I, or anyone else on the other side of the screen, listen to your words? Why should we stop and pay attention to the message that you have to bring forward?

I know it's an important message. I've been here reading your words every single day for the last 15 days. The people who are in this group are extraordinary. Can you take your extraordinary and share it in your words for why your message is important?

Here's something that came up through some of the coaching notes that I've been leaving through this challenge. One of those was talking about the "I" versus "you" versus "we." I tried to bring a message forward, but I missed the whole point of why it was important. It landed flat and confused a couple of people.

Here's the concept. If I am talking to you in a video, I just did it right there. I brought myself into the frame. I say, "Well, you know that your message is important to this world. You know that you've had the desire to get this out for an extremely long time. You know that there are people waiting to hear that message. They are waiting to hear your call because they want to heal, or they need the gift that you bring to this world. Why aren't you? I want to know why you aren't. What is it that's holding you back?"

Going through just that small piece of me just riffing at you about getting your message out, I'm talking to you, but I'm bringing myself to that frame. I don't say you and I. I don't say, "We are doing this."

I'm talking directly to you acknowledging that I am the one bringing these words forward or that these are my thoughts. It's not necessarily the thoughts of everyone because I truly don't believe that we all should believe the same thing. Our beliefs are very rooted to who we are and how we look at this world. It's the same thing that I said before. It's not tolerance. The message is important because it's for you or for your reader on the other side.

By bringing yourself into that frame, it makes it friendlier. It reminds us that there's a person carrying the message. It's not just a message. It's not someone just telling you what you should do. I hate being told what I should do or what I shouldn't do. I'd rather decide for myself.

How can you play with this concept? Why is your message important? How can you tell it directly to the person on the other side of the screen while acknowledging that this message is coming from inside of you?

It's a big challenge. I look forward to seeing what stories will come up today.

We're getting into advanced semantics here - psychologically-driven story techniques.

I'm a word weaver with wandering feet, a caregiver with instincts far beyond my practical knowledge, a campaigner for mutual respect and caring honesty.

I'm passionate about healing communication, specifically for people (like you) who are consciously working to change the world with your words.

It seems I've been granted the gift of turning dreams to reality both for myself and others, and I'm making it my mission to get these gift into the hands of those of you who are ready to voice your passions with purpose, patience, and choice.

You get to choose. You always have a choice.

And having you consciously make the choice to change HAS to happen in order for our collaboration to be successful.

My vision for my future includes being a living model of these words, where I take discovering my soul to the next level in every choice of every moment of every day to come.

Breathe in, breathe out
Breathe in
Accept what is
Manifest what could be
Breathe out
Accept what isn't
Let go of what was
Breathe in
Make room for what will be
Clear a space to accept
Breathe out
It is the way of life
Share in abundance
The tighter the hold
The quicker it slips
Go with the flow
Breathe in, breathe out
Breathe in
Breathe out

Day 16:
Do your words communicate your passion?

Yesterday I took my laptop out to dinner with me. I'm sitting there, writing a manuscript. I get to the point where I want to read some of it out loud. Mind you, I'm reading so I can barely hear my words. I'm just whispering. My hands are going, and my face is gesturing based on the emotion behind the words. A person at the table next to me says, "I don't know what you're writing, but I know it's going to be great. I can just tell because I can feel your passion."

At the same time, yesterday I started with a new client. It's someone who's coming to Write Your Book in Paradise. It was her very first coaching session with me. We had only spoken once, and that was to make sure that this was a good fit for her. In that call, she found herself sobbing through tears telling me a story that she's not really shared with anyone before. Yet, it was the heart of the message that she's wanting to share in the book that she's going to work on.

Is it alright to type through the tears? Absolutely. I've done thousands of words that way and shared many stories myself. I'd let the emotion flow. When that jug is pouring, you just let it flow. You just trust that whatever is coming out, there's a reason why it's not trickling out of the tap but pouring out of the jug.

Do your words communicate your passion? Is it enough? Think about it. See what you can add. Even if it's not the specific words, how can the mood, feel and energy of what you're creating match the moment and the need that you're bringing forward for the reader on the other side of the screen?

I totally get that you want to be sensitive to the undertones of how your information, is presented (the feeling, emotion, expression that carries your message) while also being sensitive to the overtones (what you say, how it looks, how it makes your tribe feel)

Or maybe you don't care at all - in that case you're in the wrong place.

You know what, the first thing I want you to know is that I'm going to ask you to STOP SELLING YOURSELF!

Yep, you heard me right. STOP SELLING YOURSELF. And instead let your stories, your experiences, the voice in the depth of your soul offer your gifts to the world for you.

I beg of you to answer the deep calling you feel to help people - for you to share your stories in a way that supports your business, your tribe, and betters the world...

Day 17:
Is your idea easy to understand?

Do you have a funny (or frustrating) story of when someone didn't understand your idea?

Let me start off by saying that some of you are already doing this in a magnificent way.

So much so that a woman reached out to me yesterday who's been talking to one of the people in this group for over six months.

She said, for the first time, she's really understanding what this person is about because she can hear the stories. It's making everything else make sense now that she gets the root of the story. The root is how you became the person that you are today.

Is your idea easy to understand? I know mine hasn't always been there. In the past when I talked about ghostwriting, people kept trying to hire me to write their book. They would say, "Great! I have this idea. Go research and write it for me."

No, not quite. That's not the kind of ghostwriter that I am. I'm the kind of ghostwriter that shows up and sits down next to you. Elbow to elbow, we pull all of the work out of you. Then I can go home and translate some of that work.

The reality of it is that the majority of work, if not half of it, is time spent together. This is your book, your ideas, your genius and your expertise, not mine. My gift is making sense of your expertise.

Is your idea easy to understand? If it's not, then what can you switch? When's the time that you thought you were saying it, and it really wasn't what you were doing? How can you make your idea easier to understand if it's not easy to understand already?

Truth is only as true as the moment it lives within.

My personal mission is to help heal experts' communication so their natural gifts can help others heal, grow, and learn. Oh the stories I could tell...

There was a song I heard about how we are her (mother nature's) voice and she is our song. it was on the first cd I ever owned, a gift from my grandma. And I took it as a mission after her strokes: I became her voice and she became my song.

I am always striving to deliver a clearer picture of what I have to offer. It's never static and there's always more to understand. Bit by bit, what can you share to help us understand?

Day 18:
When did you listen?

Over the last couple of weeks, we've been walking through a

process that I have. The first part of that where we went into these three-part stories and really looked at our roots is called shaping your ideas. What we just wrapped up is called organizing your actions. What we're going into is called voice your passions. Surprise, surprise, that's where my business name came from.

We're going to be going through this voice your passions piece of this three-part exercise for the next few days. The fun part about it is that you've already done all of the work.

You've looked at the roots. You've figured out how you want to position yourself, what you need to position yourself for, details that you need to include and why someone might want to listen to you. Now we're going back into story and looking at how to meld all of those ideas into one.

Today's question is, when did you listen? I don't mean did you listen to your mom, or pick up the phone and listen to someone talk to you. I mean listening to the inner wisdom that comes from within you. It could have been a mentor who said something, and it really resonated. It hit that deep core. When is it that you really listened?

One of those times for me is when I was getting ready to leave Wisconsin and move. I could move anywhere. I started researching the entire West Coast. I've lived the entire East Coast. Now it's time for me to come out west.

Though I kind of wavered on everywhere, when I started researching it, I started talking about moving to Portland. I never really felt it, but I knew some people there. I figured, why not go there?

I started having nightmares every single night. The same nightmare would come back. It would escalate and get worse. There'd be more details to go with it. It was not fun.

I sat down and had to really listen to myself. What I realized is that I was not ready to go to Portland, Los Angeles or back to a city, which is where I love to be. I also love being in the woods. I had no clue how to show up for myself in the same way that I showed up for my grandma as her caregiver and the way that I show up for my clients.

Instead I went to the Redwoods and spent a year and a half

learning to care for myself. I was really immersed in the land there. One of the things that happened is that, shortly after I moved there, I was invited to go to an Awaken Women Retreat. I went to it and had a magnificent experience. I came home and created a 100-page outline of all of my expertise.

It was like someone handed me the keys and said, "Congratulations, beautiful choice. Now go build it." I have been ever since. That was in 2015.

I'm slowly but surely ticking away at the pieces and implementing everything that lies within. When I sat down to listen, that voice got so loud that it came pouring out of me.

When did you listen?

Though I'd been asked to run a writing retreat for years, it wasn't until I attended a women's retreat that my dream turned into reality. I'm so grateful for the space that retreat facilitator held for me to LISTEN which assisted me in turning my private ghostwriting into developing the most amazing experience I could offer to a group.

Day 19:
When did you learn?

As I sat with this question this morning in meditation, I had no clue how to respond.

There are so many different ways to respond. While all the images were floating through my mind, one piece that came back is something that I hadn't really looked at in a story before. Here it goes...

I was a freshman in college taking a World Literature class. Let me tell you. In high school I was a C or D student. I was also part of 10 to 15 clubs at a time doing all sorts of things like theater and teaching art to inner city kids.

In college I realized that I was paying for this education. It wasn't just about turning in homework and getting grades. I started loving learning. I switched to become a straight A student in that very first semester in college.

In that semester, there was this woman that I had as a teacher in World Lit. I swear that she had it out for me. I would come to class a little early. I would sit and would read whatever piece of World Lit we were supposed to read. Then I would come to class and discuss it as if I had studied it.

I absorb literature. It's easy for me. I can not only read the lines, but I read between the lines. I read what's behind the words as well. I could synthesize the information, story line, plot, characters, meaning, message, moral and everything within just minutes after reading the material. My teacher was so mad. She kept trying to catch me as if I didn't know the answer. I absorbed it. I know that is one of my special skills.

I ended up leaving the education department that I started in during that semester and switched over to writing instead. I would have had to take two more classes with the same teacher. I felt that, no matter what I did, I would always be wrong, so I switched.

What I learned was that she was the best gift that I could have ever been given. I switched over to getting a writing degree. That's where I found a professor who had been a ghostwriter and had written novels. He shared all of his processes of what he did and how he brought it out. He shared the types of books he had written.

I took every class that this guy offered. I took classes that didn't interest me at all, like literature of the occult and horror lit. I could barely get through the readings. I definitely can't get through the movies because they scare me.

I now understand the psychology behind them. I understand how we create our different worlds. I have looked at it from a really broad spectrum. It was purely because I came into a class and realized that people were threatened by my intelligence.

I learned to hide that for a long, long time. I also learned to just go do what served me best. I ended up with a writing degree. I still went back to education and got an education degree. Then I got a language arts minor to support all of that.

It's not like I didn't end up where I wanted to be in the first place. It's just that the path getting there looked differently.

When did you learn? What happened? What's the story? How can you look back on that and see where it's brought you to where you are now?

I remember the exact moment I became utterly disgusted with the work I was doing and woke up to the fact that I needed to re-arrange my business priorities to get back on track. I was in the midst of a giant corporate voice rebrand for an engineering firm.

I loved it because a third of my time was spent advocating for science, technology, engineering, and math STEM education. A third of my time was spent researching green initiatives and innovations. And the final third was on engineering and architecture business stuff. Yet somehow, I went nearly a year without putting together that this was one of the top 20 engineering firms in the world and of course the majority of their money came from oil.

When the email arrived, I was at a gas station somewhere between Colorado and Utah, carsick kitties in the backseat, moving cross-country from Wisconsin to California.

The lady who was filling in for me started posting about fracking and the marketing firm that I was consulting was fired. I finished training the corporation on how to do the work in-house, washed my hands, and have been working with mindful, Earth-loving people ever since.

Moving here ripped my blinders off and I melted down at all the fluff, flash, and deception.

It's absolutely changed the way I'm showing up in my life, in business, in relationships, for myself.

Even though you don't realize it at the time, it always turns out to be exactly what you needed for a massive shift to happen.

Day 20:
When did you grow?

Let me tell you. This is pretty magical timing. Maybe he's watching the video challenge, or maybe he's not.

I received a message last night in my inbox saying, "I saw you over a year ago. You are so much more than you yet realize. Keep going. I feel as though I've watched Cinderella at the ball where she realizes her own worth and beauty. That is the moment when you, too, find your heart alive and well and truly home. Welcome home, Steph. Welcome home."

Let me just tell you how much that touched me. I remember getting up a year ago and sharing some of my personal stories. These were things that I'd not really shared with anyone before. I shared them in front of 200 people, and this man was in the audience.

I know that one of the biggest pieces that I was struggling with was not only forgiving others for some of the atrocities that I've lived through, but really learning to forgive myself. What was my normal is not normal under anyone's circumstances, nor is it acceptable.

In the process of forgiving myself, for me, it's like an artichoke. I know a lot of people use that analogy of the onion. You're pulling away each little bite of leaf as you peel your way to the center.

When you get down there, the final thing that you do is that you have to pull off all of the fuzzy choke. That's what that little fuzz is called on top of the heart. Until you get rid of your choke, there is no heart.

I know I've grown. I've watched myself reveal what was within. The way that I show up in life and the way that I do everything is completely different now. It's because I've grown. I listened and learned. I grew.

How about you? When did you grow?

Okay, okay, I get it - we're always growing! Still, what was a moment that gave you mental stretch marks?

Day 21:
When did you make someone's life a bit better?

Let me tell you. As a caregiver who has spent most of my life dedicated to other people, I never put myself first.

The first adult decision that I made for myself was moving to the Redwoods just two years ago. With everything else, there was always someone else in the forefront. There were always someone else's needs that I was considering more than my own.

When I looked at today's question this morning I thought, "Oh no. When did I make someone's life a bit better?" I found it almost hilarious because that's kind of what I'm all about.

The thought, idea and story thread that came forward was this. When I was in college, I worked at a daycare for a little while. I was that person who worked in every single room and knew every student and parent in the space. I filled in wherever was needed.

One of the times that I filled in over my spring break, I became a one-on-one aide for a four-year-old boy with autism. His regular nurse's aide had gone on vacation.

I was there. I was there every single day with him for a week. What happened in that week, less than a week, was that he became fully potty trained. This little boy was so upset to still be in diapers and have to make a mess of himself, then have to be cleaned up. He was four and really aware of it.

Every time, he would get really upset. He was talking to me. He might not have been using words. He might not have been clear, but his message was extremely obvious. Make this stop happening.

I taught him sign language. I taught him a sign to use as my hands. Instead of making the sign, he shaped my hand into the sign for bathroom and then pulled me toward the bathroom.

It was amazing. Just two or three days after we started working with this, his mom came up to me at school. She said, "I've never seen him do this. What does this mean? He keeps pulling on my hand and pulling me to the bathroom."

I said, "Your son is potty trained. He is trying to communicate with you exactly what he needs. Sometimes it's just the help with his pants or a couple of other things. He's a kid with autism. It's not all easy for him."

At least he figured out how to communicate the one thing that was upsetting him more than anything else. His mom figured it out. She then took care of it and made sure that it would happen.

Then we took a message to his school where he was most of the time. He was in part-time daycare and part-time school. Within a week, everyone, his entire universe, was understanding this one boy's request to go to the bathroom.

When is it that you made someone's life a little bit better? When was it that you saw, heard or felt something at a level that no one else was seeing, and that little bit made all the difference?

Day 22:
Why did you move forward?

You might be facing something currently. It might have been something in the past.

Why did you move forward? Why do you, every day, choose to continue to move forward in this path? What comes up for me with this question is something that's going on right now.

I decided that I was going to build a membership website. It's a big process. Up until now, about 99% of my technology has all been done by me. I've built my own websites. I've set up all of my own forms. I take care of everything. It's easy for me. I breathe it. I pick it up. I learn it a little bit, then I can run it. Doing a membership site is a little different and a lot more complicated.

A lot of things have come up in the past two weeks while I've been busy building almost 50 pages. Those 50 pages includes 22 posts and 25 pages of content on the back end of this membership site.

Why am I doing this? It's because it has nothing to do with me. There are people who have been asking me, and have been asking me for years, to get this program into their hands and make it accessible. They want me to give them the forms and templates.

My response until now has been that I don't work from templates. I don't have templates. I have spent months and months over the last year systematizing and pulling out the methodologies and formulas of exactly what I do and how I do it.

I can run through the process over and over again. I know that I'm using a very systematic process. I just didn't know what it was. I'd never seen it, and it was nothing that I could hand over.

I created it. I put all of this time in. I did a ton of work.

Then, just two days ago, the entire thing crashed. The plugins that I was using for the membership site didn't work. Nothing was connecting. No one was registering. I had to rip out my entire back end and start anew just two days ago.

Why did I move forward with this project? Why did I give up all these hours? Why do I still struggle with this? It's because I'm the person who, when I wanted a website, read some manuals and a couple of forms. I built myself a full WordPress website in a weekend. It was fully responsive, gorgeous and represented what I did. I was able to close clients off of it.

If I breathe, live and find tech easy and I have this much trouble, frustration and learning curve with doing a membership site, then what are my clients feeling?

Those clients that don't know how to put up a website or a webpage. They don't even know how to go in and edit it. I know there are some of you in here. Technology has been your overwhelm for so long that you've been in analysis paralysis and aren't doing anything.

I'm not okay with that. I'm not okay with you not getting your gifts out in this world because you're scared of a little piece of technology. I won't stand for it.

What you have to offer is so much more than who you are. It's not about you. It's about everyone that you are serving and how many people are losing out because you haven't shared your gift.

Why am I moving forward? It's because it's not about me. It's for you. I know that once I've gotten through this I will be very proud of what I've created. I know that I'm really proud of every page.

I'm proud of the way it looks and the way it's operating. I'm proud of the entire feel of the process. Is it perfect? No. Does it matter? Not really.

Why do you move forward? When did you move forward? Why are you moving forward now?

Funny how it's only my own interpretations and self-imposed limitations that create "failure". Very often, I've moved forward into something, never questioning why. It was a delicate dance between reality and hope.

I really do believe the best in people. And my instincts honed by my ancestors are far better than my doubt-filled monkey brain at making decisions. In the past, I've moved forward into what I knew I had to do even while my loved ones told me not to do it.

Fulfilling my parents' dying wishes, becoming a caregiver, writing for a living, moving to Cali - these are all things I was told not to do. Yet I chose to move forward and I'm amazed where my feet have led me.

Each of us changes the world whether consciously or not - it's how we change it that matters.

Day 23:
Did you move forward realistically?

I just had about 15 to 20 stories pop through my head sitting here at the computer, about to film. I had no clue which one to say. What was realistic? What wasn't? What did I think was realistic in the moment?

Out of all of those stories, the one that really comes forward for me is when I moved forward very realistically, very grounded in myself and had no clue what I was doing. I moved the summer before my senior year from Wisconsin to New Jersey where I knew no one.

I went from a graduating class of over 100 people to an entire school of only 100 people. It was tiny. It was not what I expected. It was very, very new. I returned to Wisconsin at the end of the year and a few months later found myself talking care of my grandma when she had 3 strokes. For a while we thought that she was doing better and that she was healing, but we found out she had just become very good at deceiving us.

During the time we thought she was doing better, I moved back to New Jersey. I got a degree in writing and worked as a professional portrait photographer in one of the largest photography companies in the nation.

What stuck out to me in that time was this: the group of friends that I had would get together at least once a week to go hear live music. One of their friends was a cover band artist. He would go and play for four or five hours at a pool hall or a restaurant.

Every week, we'd go and hang, and have a beautiful time. What I realized from that guy is that he didn't have a website. He was struggling. He was probably five or six years older than me and on a journey that I was about to head on. I had no clue that was the path I was going to take.

He and I sat down. I said, "Let me give you a bio. Let me write an article. Let me do something for you so that people can figure out who you are, what you do and you can get hired from it."

We met up. We sat down. We had a dinner. Over that dinner, I interviewed him.

I went home and wrote that interview up as a giant positioning story. I wrote it as if I were a media person who had stepped into the room and watched how much these people lit up, smiled and interacted with the musician. I wrote about how it was this giant experience he was delivering.

It turned into a one-page website that he got booked off of for the next 10 years. I insisted that we sit down to this interview. I insisted that he let me write this for him. I insisted that he let me take photographs to go with it and turn over everything to him that he needed to have a website.

Did I know what a copywriter even was at the time? No, I'd never heard the term, but I knew what I was doing. I knew that the story would deliver the experience. We showed up every single week to experience his joy, love and passion in the world which was music. This man had something special.

We became friends, and we're still friends. I returned to New Jersey when my mom died to not only be her terminal caregiver, but then take care of the estate and their dying wishes. He's the friend that was there for me the entire time, and I was there for him. And he is still one of my best friends from that era.

I'm very, very grateful that I moved forward fully realistically and had no clue what the results would possibly be.

I did know, even back in 2002 - 2003, that the only way to carry your message in a lasting sense was through your story. It's through your experiences and letting the reader feel like they're part of the experience in the moment that they're reading the words.

Do you move forward realistically? Or do you move forward with your doubts, indecisions, self-worth issues and dreams that are completely unrealistic? Did I really think I could build a membership website in three weeks? No, but I did.

I also outsourced a five-page website and paid thousands of dollars for something that I didn't need. I didn't need it because I already do it. I just didn't have confidence in my own skills. I didn't see that people had been trying to hire me for years to do this type of work. I just didn't.

How do you move forward? When did you move forward realistically?

What I often think is realistically possible is often seen as extraordinary heroics by others. It's all a matter of perspective. What's your real? When did you move forward realistically?

Day 24:
When did you move forward positively?

To the core of who I am, I'm a realistic optimist. I'm always looking and dreaming of the best possible solution that is a realistic tangible option for the dream.

Of course, I hit the end of that. Then I have to dream bigger and redesign and redesign, but that's okay. I never figured that my life would put me at where I am today. That's due to dreaming in a realistic and positive way.

When did you move forward positively? Did you move forward positively? The real root of this question is, how are your emotions affecting how you're moving forward?

For me, something big has been coming up lately. Within the last two or three weeks, every client that I have taken on or those that I've been working with for years or months have all been bringing up one word. It's a really triggering word for me. That word is God.

I grew up in a house where God was almost a forbidden word. My dad's side of the family was Jewish. My mom's side of the family was Lutheran. The grandparents went into religious wars. They both wanted us raised with their religion, and my parents said no.

They said, "You can have all of the traditions, but you can't have the religion. We're not going there. We're not forcing it on anyone." What it accidentally created was God being almost a forbidden word.

I remember coming up from my grandma's lake where my family would spend the summers. It was the grandma that I took care of after her strokes.

My aunt was sitting and reading with her two children. I watched her beat her child with this book. I didn't know what was going on.

We were told, "Don't interfere."

It was the Bible. She was literally beating the Bible into her children.

This was my introduction to organized religion.

Those triggers around the word God dissolved as I gained greater knowledge of the religions of the world.

What I see is beauty, miracles, joy, love, appreciation, and gratitude. That's all I can ask for. It's MORE than I could ask for.

My religious and spiritual clients are people I love working with. They are moving forward positively. They're moving forward realistically.

How is it that you move forward? I could have said, "Nope, I don't want to work with you. We're not talking about God and religion. I don't go there. I'm sorry. We're not a fit. Go away." The reality is that it's just a word.

When did you move forward positively? Or when didn't you? How has that affected where you are now?

You know that feeling in between creating something massive
and then telling the world about it?
That moment of doubt.
Of paralyzing fear.
Will they like it?
Is it good enough?
That moment of regret.
Of pied piper whispers.
"No one's going to want it.
It isn't going to help anyone."
That moment of sheer panic.
Of pitiful self-judgement.
"Should I even launch now that they're doing the same thing.
They're going to do it better, faster, and prettier."
That moment of self-sabotage.
Of punishing yourself with comparing and competing.
And then you take a deep breath.
You remember it isn't about you, it's about them.
And then you tell the world.

Day 25:
What did you appreciate in the journey?

When I say "journey," a couple of things came up. There's the journey of life, a specific little journey or a trip that I took. What do I mean?

You get to choose which you want to talk about and what you appreciated in that journey. Maybe you can write about them all over the next few days. The journey that I'm looking at is being a caregiver for someone else's family. It's a story that I very rarely talk about. I don't know if I've ever shared it publicly.

Let me tell you that I'm on take ten or eleven right now because it's hard. It's hard to tell a story that you've never told before whether that's verbally or in writing. When it's still living inside of you, before it's anything that is tangible to someone else, that's that magic moment when you get to decide how the words are going to come out.

What did I appreciate in the journey? The journey for me is a journey that I took to Wyoming. I spent a month living right outside of the east gate to the entrance of Yellowstone. I was living with a guy at the time. His father had been out on a cross country motorcycle trip. He was rear-ended by another motorcyclist on the trip. It was bad. It was ugly.

Spoiler alert: Everyone was perfectly safe and fine and put back together in the end. Humpty Dumpty will live to see another day.

It was a very intense time. My boyfriend at the time and I lived in a little inn a couple of blocks from the hospital. We could walk over every day and take care of every single thing that the Dad needed.

His dad, however, was getting worse every day. The treatments weren't working. He was needing more surgeries. He needed to get out of this little town in the middle of nowhere and get to a big hospital. Insurance wouldn't cover it. Insurance wouldn't cover anything other than just the basic care.

I ended up putting money up. We found an angel investor pilot community. They brought in an air ambulance and air-lifted him back to Wisconsin. The hospital that I bought my house a couple of blocks from so that I could take care of grandma was one of the top two trauma centers in the world.

Insurance wouldn't cover it unless both the doctor from Wyoming and the doctor who received the patient in Wisconsin said yes. Then insurance would pay for it. When you're working with a pilot, they kind of want their money up front. What are you to do?

Every time it was Dad's nap time or Nurse-Doctor time, my boyfriend and I would get into the car and drive to Yellowstone.

We did things like driving through herds of cattle and finding off-roading paths through the creeks and mountains where we lived. Every single time that we knew that we had at least two hours where we knew that we could not do anything. That moment when you just feel helpless because there's nothing to do.

In those moments, we went out and appreciated the journey. We were not happy because of why we were there. What we were doing was not fun. We appreciated the journey. Sometimes we'd cry while driving through Yellowstone going to see the geysers. Driving through the herd of buffalo was one of the coolest things.

They'd been air-lifted out. My boyfriend went with his dad in the plane. I drove back the truck and all of the family belongings. While I was driving, not in my car or with my stuff, I came across a moose. It was not even 10 feet off of the road, munching away.

It had just started to snow. It was way up in the mountains. The road was dusted with white. There was a moose. He was so warm that he was steaming, which is actually what caught my attention. Otherwise, I don't know that I would have seen it.

The white snow and the steaming moose eating grass was the coolest thing ever. That topped the cake for me. That's how I said farewell to a month of caregiving for someone else in Wyoming.

It was a beautiful journey even though what I needed to do and what was asked of me on that journey was very intense. I really appreciated the journey, the experience and that opportunity for a time in my life that I never would have had otherwise.

What did you appreciate in the journey? What supported you? When you were in some of the heaviest trials and tribulations in your life, could you appreciate the moment looking back?

When have you pushed yourself to step outside of your comfort zone... and found yourself more comfortable than you expected?

Day 26:
What truth can you brag?

What's little in your eyes is often awe-inspiring in your community and your tribe's eyes. They had no clue that, what you did, they could do for themselves. It's merely making a choice to move forward.

What is it that you can brag about? What truth does no one know about because you feel like you're bragging?

You're not just telling the truth. You're sharing with someone who doesn't know you or what you've experienced. They don't know you from anyone and they want to feel what you've felt. How can you invite them into the experience and brag a little bit? Just claim your credibility.

When I look at this, the first thing that comes forward to me is return on intention. Yes, your return on investment is very important, but you can't get that without setting an intention.

Helping my clients get extraordinary results with their ROI, return on intention, has been one of the specialties that I've had. Let me tell you, I am not money driven. If I could give this away every single day, I would. However, I have a life and a house and a couple of things that need paid for. Money helps me deliver to you even better.

When I look back at my clients, I had a client come to me who said that her number one goal was to be able to heal as many people as possible. She came to me to write a website. After our work together, she went from talking to a couple hundred people every few months to an online radio audience of 100,000 people.

I did a voice rebrand for a corporation that was so distinct and clear that it was written up in Wikipedia. I can find their brand, including their voice brand, online even though I can't say which corporation I was working for.

Then you take other entrepreneurs who hire me for one session where we repositioned his program value and he immediately enrolled someone who is an extraordinarily perfect fit. They were able to self-select into his work.

There are other people, like a ghostwriting client who hired me to do a one-on-one five-day retreat with him in the Redwoods. He had three very separate businesses. They were all being run by different people. The only common denominator was that, with all three businesses, their websites had been built by the same designer. Other than that, you couldn't tell that the brands were related.

We branded him, the captain of these three businesses. We created a voice key. There is a universal language that any of the people can use working in the businesses, putting up the blog content, posting and sharing. There is a universal language for everyone to use that is pre-approved by the person who is being represented.

He is the one who came to me and said, "I cannot believe how helpful that phraseology key is going to be. Thank you, Steph! Will you come back?" I'm heading back up to do some more work with him for his team and to train his community on what it means to write to convert, how that shows up on your website, how you write your signature talk, and how you create a positioning story for yourself that's going to last longer than two days or six months, but be something that you're growing into for the next 10 years.

Then I have clients that I worked with 10 years ago that are coming to me saying, "We're finally there. I've grown into it all."

I have times that can make me feel like a failure. Years ago, I set five massive plans for a five-year goal. Three of those pieces are done. Two of them are in progress. Everything is happening. But, yes, I can feel like I'm failing at times.

It was a five-year plan, Steph. And you're doing it. What you're doing had such vision back then that it is exactly where you're going now. That's something to brag about. I knew myself so well that I just knew I needed time to step into it. I could design something like that for myself. It's awesome that I get to do the same thing for clients who, year after year, still see the results from the work that we did.

That's my truth. That's not me bragging. That's not my ego talking. That's just where they've been, where they are now and the feedback that they've given me. It's just what I've done.

I know that you have done a lot, too. So, what is it that you did that doesn't seem like anything to you but is truly extraordinary to the person on the other side who hasn't even taken the first step on that path to seeing what they see in you?

How can you claim? How can you brag? What is it that we don't know about you but would really change our understanding of who you are at a very deep level?

Day 27:

How have you followed the current of your unique purpose?

After my senior year of high school, I moved across the country from New Jersey back to Wisconsin to be near the rest of my family and fulfill a contract as a YMCA summer camp counselor. I wanted and needed some time off instead of going straight to college.

When it came close to graduation, I knew, not only was I not supposed to be in college, but I was supposed to be back in Wisconsin. I arranged everything, because I had a contract to work for the summer, to graduate my senior year three weeks ahead of everyone else. I finished my course work, got on a plane and went to Wisconsin.

I was one of two people in my graduating class that didn't go to college. It was big deal to take a break between high school and college. Now, it's a little more acceptable, but then, not so much.

In that very first semester that I took off between high school and college, I got my driver's license. I'd always lived in metropolitan areas and never needed it. My grandma was insistent. "You have to get your license." She took me driving. She took me for my test. I got my license.

What would have been that first semester is when my grandma had her three strokes. When I became a caregiver. When I found my grandma on the floor at the foot of my door and had to figure out how to get her 4'11" 200 pounds off the ground with half of her body numb and both of her knees supposed to be replaced that winter.

It was one of the most intense moments of my life. At the time, I was 18. I had not really experienced anything like that. In that moment, it was so obvious to me that that's why I wasn't in school. That's why I felt so pulled to return to Wisconsin, to be there for her.

It was stepping out into nature. After getting her off the floor, I got her to the bathroom so she could dress herself while seated but trapped between the counter and the wall. In those couple of minutes, I ran outside to think, "What is going on? Why me? What am I supposed to do?"

As soon as I walked outside, you couldn't hear anything, other than snowflakes hitting snow. It had snowed over two feet overnight already, and more was coming down. The snowflakes were so big that you could see their entire crystalline structure, each one different from the next.

In that moment, it was like getting a download. Push broom. Shovel. Pitchfork. What? Alright. Here we go, off and running. No problem. A two-minute break, and I had complete clarity of what I was supposed to do.

I grabbed the push broom and cleared all of the snow off the car. I shoved the pitchfork in the very front of the grass and pulled the car all the way forward. I shoveled a path to the door. I went and got my grandma from the bathroom. I walked behind her like a human wheelchair, lifting each side as we walked her forward.

I got her in the car. I got her to the hospital, a place that I had never driven to. I didn't know the road names. I kept her alive and I kept her awake. It was an hour drive to the hospital. I somehow got her there in less than an hour. It was just extraordinary how every piece of the puzzle happened that day.

In that car ride, my grandma started sharing with me all the family secrets. The stories that I didn't know. The stories that would add perspective, compassion and understanding – stories that she really didn't want to die with her.

My mom pre-deceased my grandma, so it's not like she was sharing those stories. But my grandma took that hour to tell me everything. Her brain was still going. It was some of the very recent stuff. All of those secret stories is how I kept her mind engaged and active on the way to the hospital.

Then I became her voice. She was my song. I spent years with her. She was my everything. That moment and what came forward, and what it was like to be with her, is what led me to help be a voice for so many other people. It led me to encourage all of you to share your songs and your stories, and to give voice to what we wouldn't know otherwise.

I woke up this morning to find out that one of my friends from childhood had lost the battle with cancer. It's emotional. But he and I had this talk over and over again. He did it. He shared his voice very loudly and very clearly. All I can ask is that you do the same.

How have you followed the current of your unique purpose? What is it that brought you here? How have you just known? What is it that you were going to face, and you just knew what you were supposed to do? You knew that this was given to you for a very specific purpose. The things that you didn't plan, but kind of pushed you on that inner tube down the river.

Day 28:
What are the puzzle pieces that make you uniquely and authentically you?

To be honest, it was this question that spurred me to create the course, Writing That Converts. I looked at all of the different pieces that are just me. They are so me that I didn't even see that I was doing them until other people started telling me. I've always just done it.

These are things that I just know how to do, I've always known how to do. No one had to tell me or teach me. I was able to take practical knowledge from life and reapply it into that forum. Some of those things would be copywriting, editing, book projects, voice branding and marketing. It's just who I am. It's always been easy for me.

That's where this program came from. Writing That Converts was me trying to figure out my natural systems. A book project to me isn't just a book. It's the process of writing the book, interviewing it out of you, doing a collaboration where we're literally working elbow to elbow to make this book happen. I'm not the ghostwriter where you're saying, "Here are 100 pages. Go do it." I'm a different type. This is a type that listens, pulls, translates and word weaves with you.

When I looked at a book project, it was never just a book text. In the process of writing that book, you'd end up with articles that you could use to preview it. You'd usually end up with copywriting. I always looked at, how is this book supporting you and your business?

I very rarely worked outside of the business realm. My specialty and goal is, how do you position your expertise in a way that others can understand your credibility? It's not fabrication. I cannot make you an expert.

What I can do is help you to find your unique points and your authenticity, and to bring that out in all ways of communication. The strongest way to do that is with stories.

That's how the course was born. That's a huge chunk of the puzzle pieces. Those are big puzzle pieces that make me uniquely and authentically me in the way that I'm showing up in my business.

Of course, I can answer this question in my life, in relationships and in so many other ways. But I'm very focused with just this one question. How is it related to your business? This is the key for me, over and over again. I always go through the entire program, but as I get to the end, I realize that's how I can put it together.

I can take these five different puzzle pieces and, shazam, you have access to everything that's inside of my brain. At least the first go-round of trying to get it out. This has been a year in the making.

What is it that makes you uniquely and authentically you? How have you brought yourself forward in a way that is so you that you can't even make sense of it half the time for other people? It's just how you operate in this world.

My role is to make the words on your website make sense of who you are, what you do, and what you're offering for your tribe in a way that they understand the value you can deliver.

How can you deliver the message and change the focus from yourself to what is the value you bring to your audience? What are the distractions that keep you from getting your message out?

Day 29:
What terms accurately describe where you've been and what you're doing in a way that makes sense to your community?

I personally have struggled with titles, terminology and what to call myself since moving online. I have called myself a ghostwriter, a copywriter, a marketer, a content brander, a voice brander. I can keep going. They are all kind of meaningless because I do all of it.

So, how can you pick one phase when you do it all? When the industry looks at these as all different things, and you only see it as one project. That's where it's been really tricky for me.

Last year, I walked into an event. I came in a few minutes late because I was working with one of the other staff members privately before coming back to the event. I walked in and they were in the middle of an exercise, introducing themselves to the room through a metaphor. I was put in the spotlight. I never even sat down. It was, "Welcome, Steph. Introduce yourself. Pick a metaphor. Go."

What came out was a metaphor of a tapestry, pulling your thought threads out and weaving your words together to create an entire image and story. You see those old tapestries. If you go to the cloisters in New York, you see the unicorns. You see the men in armor in these gorgeous, old tapestries. What I see when I look at those is that, everything about these tapestries inspires strength, and yet it reflects grace in everything that's there. The way that I look at word weaving and story pulling your thought threads is similar to creating a tapestry. Something that seems like it's just black, white, yellow or red. But, as soon as they start coming together, it becomes a kaleidoscope of color, of understanding. A true message can come through what was once just wisps of thought.

What is it that you do? Where have you been? How did the terms that make sense with that come together to explain who you are in a way that makes sense to your community?

Day 30:
How does your journey parallel what your ideal clients are walking?

Where are they now? What path or journey are they following? How have you already been there? How have you already taken a very similar or parallel journey? What journey was it?

When I look at the journey of this last 30 days, we all took off masks and started showing deeper levels of ourselves to everyone else. We all grew and started to transform, whether it was transformation from within, transforming the words coming out of our mouth, or transforming the audiences where you're sharing your words. We have cried. We have laughed. We have acknowledged our emotions, the way we feel and how it affects our mood and everything else around us through story. We have moved forward together. Just as I took time to find my voice, to create the products, to grow my business in a way that I can serve the people that I want to serve, and the people that want to work with me. How amazing that we get to choose each other now! I can only assume that you want the same.

I was talking to this internet marketer in Australia. She came to California and did an event recently. One of the things that we talked about was how she took on a private client for some really high-end work. It wasn't a good fit. Even in the enrollment, she knew it wasn't quite right, but she said yes and they moved forward. It left such a tainted taste in her mouth that she stopped working one on one for a while.

And I've learned that lesson this past year, too, working with some not-right-fit people. You get to choose who you want to work with, always. You get to choose which foot you're going to step on which path, and when. You get to design the life that you want for yourself. It can be really easy and effortless, as long as you stay here. As long as you stay in your heart, you can have it all.

That's how I feel that you are walking the path that I already have walked before. Some of you might be on this path already with me. We're just showing up in different ways. There is that phrase, "A rising tide lifts all boats." Well, let's sail the seas together.

So, how is it that your journey is mirroring your clients'? How does the parallel look? What is the parallel? How can you show us?

Day 31:
The day after...

Just because we're at the end of the 30-day challenge doesn't mean that our relationship is over. Are you still planning to write today?

If you were brave enough to face this challenge along with me, head to www.stephritz.com for a free follow up call.

The 4 A's of Authenticity in Marketing
(Writing Exercise)

Your experiences put you in a position of authority, growth, leadership, and expertise, as well as show others how you became an expert at what you offer the world.

It comes down to:

- How you communicate
- Personality
- Name and reputation
- Honesty and integrity
- Being your own advocate

You have to create a road to opportunity – to pave the way for others to rise to their own highest awareness and inner guidance. Story is the best way to show gratitude for the very personal insights life has offered you on your path to today. Explaining what you can do and what you love to do through story allows others to see your passions like a sticky note stuck to your forehead.

Authenticity in Marketing (THEM)

1. What solution will they *agree* is right for them?
2. What can you *assume* they already know?
3. What might you say that they'd *argue*?
4. What is their biggest *aspiration*?

Authenticity in Marketing (YOU)

1. What do they need to *agree* to move forward?
2. What are they already *assuming* about you?
3. What does voice fear *argue* against you?
4. What do they see in you that they are *aspiring* to become?

Authenticity in Conversion Communication

1. What *actions* do you want them to take?
2. What fresh *awareness* can you bring to their current knowledge?
3. What value are they ready to *accept* from you?
4. What do they want to *accomplish*?

~~~

Steph really does take people to a 5th dimension of thinking!

~ Dr. Stephen Steiner,
CEO Aerogel Technologies & NASA scientist,
(6th grade friend who introduced Steph to Forensics)

~~~

Steph suggested I bring more of myself to the project – a revelation in making my project more personal and more accessible to my readers. She was exactly the right person to help me.

~ Debbie Howard
#1 Bestselling Amazon author & TedX Tokyo speaker

~~~

Steph is not only an organization wiz but also a fabulous writer goddess. She holds sacred space for me to become comfortable expressing my truth in written form. She pulls words out of me that are the future, so I can live into the writing.

~ Meilin Ehlke, Shamanic Energy Artist

~~~

Poetry: A Sacred Portal for Healing
Michelle Bee, LMFT

Long before there were social workers or other helping professionals, poets and storytellers helped people deal with their deepest fears by echoing the struggles of humanity in their poems, myths, and stories (Harrower, 1972).

Michelle Bee is a multi-ethnic, intuitive poet and psychotherapist. Truly a unique healing voice that stands out in the therapy world. Healing with the use of liberation tools like poetry, journaling, storytelling and song. Deep rooted in restoring biorhythms with movement, EFT tapping, and personal self-love practices. Her work is grounded in life visioning, affirmative prayer, meditation and the creation of spiritual rituals.

As an ease-based alchemist, she explores the elements needed to transform the heaviness of systematic life into gold star dust.

Michelle says, "The more we release, the higher we can rise." She practices this process with her own life by identifying and releasing thoughts, emotions and habits that came from societal programming to expose her truest self. Her goal is to embrace a more liberated view of herself, her body, and her life path.

Using her love for poetry and therapeutic writing, she has created two books, Searching for SHE and 33 Days of Healing Words. She has also been published in The Seed of Destiny, sharing stories, poems and prayers.

Her 10 years as a licensed psychotherapist centers around emotional release work, social-emotional wellness, identity root work and the mastery of self-love, self-trust and self-care practices.

As a poet and psychotherapist, Michelle Bee knows the healing power of poetry and writing. Before becoming a licensed therapist, she was using poetry and journaling to make sense of her world and early childhood experiences. It became Michelle's main tool for expressing deep feelings and emotions, processing trauma and finding her voice.

This chapter is an invitation for you to explore poetry, literature and journaling as a portal of self-discovery. A new way to view life challenges, thoughts and emotions.

On this journey, the goal is to develop creative ways to manage life transitions, express yourself and spark new insights with poetry and transformative writing tools.

It is Michelle's intention that this process opens new doors of mindful awareness, self-understanding, inspired problem solving and a technique for integrating parts of yourself that seems to be at odds.

Michelle's ability to facilitate a safe space for self-healing is extraordinary. Though people see me showing up differently, no one really knows what's causing the shift.... a gut-wrenching awakening is what. It's like I can feel the roots growing out of my feet, grounding me deeper and stronger, holding me steady as I let the sweet sap of inner knowing pour out of me... Intense. Grateful. ~ Steph Ritz

---

The Journey into Self

Smell the flowers little one

Be in the beauty of

Your inner blossoming

Long before I knew the rich history or science behind it, I was using pen and paper to heal. When I felt intense emotions and had no one to share them with, I could tell them to the page and something about that felt liberating.

I remember doing this as early as second grade, with my sloppy handwriting that slanted below the lines on the pages of my secret diary with a built-in lock and key that I kept hidden.

I remember buying the diary at our school book fair which included a pop-up shop with journals, pens and stationery for sale. Even though the lock was flimsy, and anyone with a strong grip could tug it open, I trusted it to keep my secrets.

My journal was my friend; after school I would share my frustration, my heart ache, who I liked and didn't like, how I wished I had different parents, and how sometimes I wished I was never born. Getting it all out meant I wasn't carrying it around; when it hit the page, I could let it go.

That is the power of telling your story.

Somewhere around third grade I was introduced to formal poetry through a lesson plan on famous poets and their poems. Up until then my knowledge of poetry was nursery rhymes, Dr. Seuss, and the Hip-Hop played by my older siblings. Somehow the poems of authors like Maya Angelou felt deeper, they opened an intimate portal into the human soul. The poetry genre drew all my attention. They were telling honest stories of pain, love, and life in a short form with magnificent metaphors that made me feel it, relate to it, and want more and more of it.

I would go to the library and feel the magnetic pull to walk quickly, but quietly, to the poetry section. Checking out stacks of books at a time, I would find a quiet space to crack them open and cross over into new dimensions of intimacy and self-reflection. It felt like I was reading their secret diary and sometimes I could see myself in their words.

The rhyme schemes felt like words with a heartbeat, and together they made a living-breathing song. What a lovely way to tell a story. An art form of words, story and all the emotional hues of humanity. I started writing poems to express my emotions and experiences. This mesmerizing lyrical form allowed me to make beauty out of pain and celebrate my unique interpretation of life.

Taking my time to create and organize my thoughts and feelings into a poem allowed me to work it out, like molding clay with words until a sculptured form appeared.

True poetry is more than words or rhymes; in its purest form, it is a living organism. When you come into contact with poetic substance there is movement. Subconscious thoughts, visions, and sensations arise. Ideas emerge and feelings appear in response to the poetic substance.

Here your true inner beliefs are expose. Warning: things within you may surface, evaporate, expand and change form. Surrender to it. Allow the medicinal power of poetry to guide you to the truth. Be willing to look, and look again. I encourage you to use the poetic process as a method to understand the world around you, within you and beyond you.

Poetry Therapy

"Poetry Therapy, or poetry which is used for healing and personal growth, may be traced back to ancient times when religious rites in which shamans and witch doctors chanted poetry for the well-being of the tribe or individual." – National Association for Poetry Therapy

Poetry is an ancient and complex human art form used for education, prescribed as medication, designed for elevation, and entertainment. Its rhythmic song is a magic spell on the mind and creates easy recall and deep access to the memory centers of the brain.

As a psychotherapist and poet, I use poetry therapy to help clients explore, accept and express who they are. The purpose of this process is to release the mask commonly used to fit in to society; to dive deep into the depths of self to unlock curiosity, authenticity and self-expression. According to the National Association for Poetry Therapy (NAPT), the healing practice of poetry therapy has roots as far back as the fourth millennium BCE in ancient Egypt.

The use of poems with purpose allows the reflecting and processing of deep emotions and ideas. Studies on poetry and healing have noted the benefits of reading, listening to and writing poetry. These benefits include reduction in pain, fear, sadness, anger, worry and fatigue.

"Poetry can take the most extreme emotions and bottle them like tinctures that can be used to heal the reader; it is expression-giving a voice to that which we need as human beings to express, that gives poetry its strong influence." - Nicole Bouchard

As a Poetry Therapist, I skillfully identify poems and other art forms for my client's and prescribe them as part of the treatment and healing process.

Poetry therapy can incorporate music, art, meditation and movement to enhance creativity and the examination of therapeutic themes and ideas. I believe one of the essential elements of this process is the reflective writing.

Research by Dr. Pennebaker, a social psychologist, found that writing about emotions and stress can boost immune functioning and help with mental and physical wellbeing by decreasing anxiety, blood pressure, depression, muscle tension, pain and stress. His research also revealed enhanced lung and immune function.

According to Good Therapy, poetry therapy is practiced internationally by hundreds of professionals, including psychotherapists, psychologists, psychiatrists, counselors, social workers, educators and librarians.

The approach has been used successfully in a number of settings— community counseling centers, therapy offices, schools, libraries, hospitals, rehabilitation centers, and correctional institutions, to name a few.

This chapter is an introduction to my personal use of poetry for healing and my ability to incorporate this into my professional work. This is not a replacement for working with a mental health professional to address psychological, social or emotional distress.

Diving Deep

Poetry is a tool for exploring the hidden crevasses of ourselves and our human existence. It is a safe and private journey which doesn't require sharing, unless you choose to. It's beautiful use of metaphors, symbols and creative liberties allow it to have a dream like quality of making sense of non-sense or simply being perplexed and having a love affair with contemplating its meaning. That is the purpose of creating art, to contemplate and consider the possibilities.

Many specks of dust,
stuck to my ribs
like stars affixed
to the night sky.

I wanted them to go,
I wanted clear space.

But what is the sky
Without sun, moon,
Or stars?

Without the moving of clouds
Ushering in a constant flow
Of infinite shapes,
A rotation of space,
Air, water, fire and dust.

Poetry has a natural way of looking at things from many different angles. A way of noticing we are doing a balancing act to simultaneously walk in many worlds. The human existence is the journey of the ever-evolving self and the worlds we move through, navigating the allure to leave parts of us behind to belong. The universe knows we are clouded by the paradox of true self and belonging. The reality is, we can only belong to ourselves.

We are tethered together
both body and spirit,
flesh and mystery,
this is the primal relationship,
a creation of heaven and earth,

a vast wind of change,
a morning sunrise,
a shifting tide,
a running wolf,
a snowcapped mountain,
a peaceful stillness.

Together we will explore the use of words, poems and prayers to unlock and open your windows, doors, and heart. To let fresh air flow like freedom, grace, and ease.

If there is one thing you hear, hear this: poetry heals. You can develop a poetry practice that is transformational. The steps below describe some ways you can connect with poetry for healing. I invite you to explore this poetic process as a pathway to better mental, physical, spiritual and emotional well-being.

Step One:
Read the poem. If you read it out loud, it improves processing and comprehension.

Step Two:
Write a response. You can use the writing prompts provided as a supportive tool.

Step Three:
Reflect. Take a moment to read what you wrote and write a reflection. Contemplate your thoughts, feelings, and beliefs about what you wrote.

Journaling with Poems

My Peace

Spiritual peace came in the form of blackness
From shaded trees, rooted in serene tranquility;
From the cool calm of the satin breeze,
No bright lights or flashy things,
Only blended gray to the deepest black.

Writing Prompt: What comes to mind when you think about peace?

Release Me

I am caught between yesterday and today
Wedged like a pebble beneath a flowing stream
Longing to be released to flow
Free

Writing Prompt: Where do you feel stuck in life right now?

Tea Time

I'm a tea kettle full of steam;
I climax with a melodic moan—
My cup runneth over.

Writing Prompt: Describe something that feels pleasurable in as much detail as possible.

Unity

I want to swim in the ocean with you,

Naked.

I want to lie in the sweet spring grass and laugh for hours—

Escape.

I want to kiss under falling rain in sunlight ...

Rainbow.

Writing Prompt: List three moments you want to create to feel a deeper connection with someone.

Dance

When I dance,
the day breaks
into existence,
the waves crash
with bravery and certainty,
life's cup runneth over, and
sea birds glide
down playground slides
and smile.

Writing Prompt: How do you feel when you dance?

Life Span

Oh my dear,
You are a rooted tree.
Your rings track the years.
Your seasons are many.
Leaves have fallen and
new growth followed.

Do not live only for Spring.
Be eternal.
Live for the sake of living.

Writing Prompt: What season of life are you in? How would
you describe it?

Why the Flowers Persist

You, dear flower
Persist
Beyond trampling steps
of unmindful feet
Past heavy rains
In abandoned fields
Buried under concrete

A forgotten garden—
Yet blooming
Persists

You are made of lichen
That which lives on
Earth and in Space
Between this time, and
Another time

In stone, trees and water
You exhale your seeds
To the air
And they spread

No one, no thing
Can stop you
Generation after generation
You
Persist.

Writing Prompt: What makes you persist even when things feel stacked up against you?

Ancestor

His face was a map,
Trails, twists, turns, choices
All the ancestor's voices exist
With his vibratory breath

His brow straight –
Able to navigate
The spinning circles
Around the lies
That sound like they might
Be true

He says, "So It Is" and
"I Love You"

Writing Prompt: What do your ancestors says?

Tense

Clenched jaw –
Teeth harshly pressed
Together

Pressure radiates-
Head, neck, shoulders,
back.
Back –
It's behind you.
You can let go
You can relax.

Writing Prompt: What is something in your past that you want to let go of?

Wounded Heart

Deep green heart
Heavy with layers
Healing surface scratches
With thin scabs
Soon they will flake away
Revealing a Healed
Healthy, Thriving
Abyss of Love.

Writing Prompt: How do you heal a wounded heart?

Woman of the Water & Wind

She moves as many things,

Water, air, clouds, fog

She exists in non-physical spaces,

In places of mystical substance –

Here-she-is able to do/be –

Integrated with the Creative Force of

Movement, flow, power,

Trust, knowing, wisdom,

Flow, flow, trust

It is so – so-

Move

in the "Unmovable."

Writing Prompt: When have you moved something forward
that felt unmovable?

Poetry as Mindfulness Practice

There comes a time
For sweet vulnerability
An open-ness to
Falling apart, to
Releasing petals
That have absorbed
All of the rain and heat
Joy and pain
Completely ready to
Surrender

Welcome in the soft and quiet
Moment
Welcome in the final wither
Allow a reverential bow
To nature
Taking her course

Writing Prompt: How have you honored the natural
transitions from season to season?

Fitting In

Find your box, and get in it.
Hurry—there isn't much time.
If you wait too long, you will be all alone.

Break limbs to squeeze in.

There may be parts that don't fit,
But you can cut them off,
Like in the Brothers Grimm.
You can remove a heel or a toe;
Shhhh... they don't have to know.

Remember it's for the promise
Of fitting into a glass slipper,
To marry a prince—
It's like that.

Squeeze in, tighter and tighter.
Hold your breath.
It's okay if you lose circulation
And parts go numb—
Don't worry about that.

All that matters is you're in.
Now you belong.
Don't you feel better?

Writing Prompt: What have you sacrificed to "fit in?"

Fake Identity

Don't open my pocketbook
I got ten fake ID's
Ten ways to please

I sometimes disassociate
The other nine
Tying to play one role at a time

But I get dizzy
Circles within circles
Switching the codes
Locking myself out

How do I get in
Where do I fit in

One day I'll throw them all away
And stand naked
in front of the still morning
A stranger to myself

Until something familiar in the sunrise
Warms my skin
And I smile,
"I know you."

Writing Prompt: Where in your life are you pretending? Where
are you authentically you?

Yes, I am Broken

Yes, be defective in the unjust system...
Be broken,
Do not fit in,
Be angry,
Be a voice of upheaval,
Do not encounter evil and smile.

Cross the street,
When the mic comes to you- object
When they light the gas, use the extinguisher of truth
Be of good measure
Measure yourself with your soul.

Wear your red, when the dress code is white
Put down the shovel,
Stop digging and Resist
Resist with Rest,

Beautiful, Rest
Stretched out, Rest
Taking up the whole space, Rest
Let your soft body open,
Spreading itself across the sheets,
And Rest.

Writing Prompt: List 55 ways to rest.

Advice for the Fearful

Worry is a cancer,
so don't stand still
Dance,
Laugh,
Tell a joke (to yourself in a whisper)
Scream out loud
Tell the people you love – "I LOVE YOU!"
Ask for a hug
Save someone, even if that someone is you
Tap your foot to the beat
Shake your hands like beautiful fans of silk and parchment
Paint them with watercolors flowing in patterns and lines
Shake yourself free
Do it from the heart
Sing from the belly
Let go
Life is in the now moment
So be here
Let the winds sway you
In the direction you are meant to travel
Listen,
Do you feel it calling to you?
It's saying,
Don't worry,
I've got a plan for you-
And it's a good one

Writing Prompt: What advice do you have for yourself to
overcome fear and worry?

Trance of the Outer World Dance

I run for the door at the end of the corridor—

A metaphor for freedom—

But it's a hallucination:

Always moving farther from my grasp

Even when I run.

I feel I'll come undone:

It mocks me,

Taunts me,

Haunts me,

Yet I can't walk away—

Even though it's no life for me to stay.

A diluted, yet shared, state of being,

All being deceived,

All fearing to leave ...

There's no love in fear;

There's no love in here.

It's not outside but deep within,

The journey home to love again.

Writing Prompt: Write about your journey home to love.

Warrior Woman

A rose can grow upward,
 from under hard dirt,
dry dirt,
pure stone.

So long as she's brave,
courageous,
and embracing
her power.

To grown
from the bottom
of callused feet,
under the waves,
under the hot sun.

If a Lotus lives its dream,
it can expose its petals,
releasing fragrance,
blossoming beautifully
from its own desire to open.

Opening to softness,
to rain kisses,
to the breeze,
to love.

Writing Prompt: How have you been brave and courageous
in life? What do you desire to open up to?

Sun in Winter

Fire and Ice
dance together
all day long

moments of break-throughs
melt-downs, holding steady,
sinking, rising, turning

brightness with stillness
peach and yellow-orange
against winter white

artistic lovers,
each aware of
the others
position

each a solo
and a
solar-system.

Writing Prompt: Where are you hot and cold at the same
time?

Work with Michelle

www.MichelleBee.com

Are you a passionate person who is...

- Wanting to integrate a solid self-care routine to energize you throughout your day?

- Looking to learn the skills required to move forward in your career with integrity and a strong sense of intention?

- Excited about your future opportunities and ready to explore a creative business strategy?

- Ready to receive personalized guidance as you manage life transitions and process you personal responses to stress?

- Eager to join a supportive community to develop your unique voice?

Take action to transform your world! As a master guide, I will support you through the process. You deserve to...

- Know the values, philosophies and practices required for your optimal health.

- Find ease in making decisions and expressing your voice.

- Receive prosperity and joy as you express your gifts and talents at work.

- Experience an abundance of positive energy every day.

It would be my joy to become part of your professional support system. I'm a practicing Licensed Marriage and Family Therapist and an Approved Clinical Supervisor, with fifteen years of clinical and educational experience. I have worked with diverse populations birth through adulthood. I am passionate about including the arts into supervision and the therapeutic process. I currently serve as the Expressive Arts Committee co-chair for the Los Angeles Marriage and Family Therapist Association.

Poetry Healing Sessions

If there is one thing you hear, hear this: poetry heals. Poets and philosophers have been aware of the curative and healing nature of poetry for millennia. Long before there were social workers or other helping professionals, poets and storytellers helped people deal with their deepest fears by echoing the struggles of humanity in their poems, myths, and stories (Harrower, 1972).

- Experience this creative process for yourself in a group of link minded souls or in private one-on-one sessions that are healing, creative and fun?

- Do you like poetry? Do you enjoy creative play time with other visionaries, writers, and healers?

- If you said yes, then poetry healing sessions are for you!

- Learn to use the therapeutic power of poetry, song, video/movie clips, images, literature, movement and other creative arts to transform your life.

- Explore deep-seated emotions, process trauma, manage stress, and learn artistic ways to cope with anxiety and depression.

Groups:

Come join an intimate group of women who love poetry, connection, mindful reflection and writing! Each group is a special gathering of souls and a magical constellation never to be repeated again.

Private Individual Sessions:

Are you feeling stuck with traditional coaching or therapy? It might be time to try something new.

Weekly Planning

Do you want weekly support and accountability? Join our weekly planning group! We meet virtually, in a loving space to reflect on aligned goals and get organized for a successful week. Get back on track with managing your goals and organizing your life! Let's touch base and see if a weekly planning session can help.

Therapy

Individual and group therapy sessions are available. Please schedule a free chat to see if this is right for you.

Words as Medicine

Individual and group sessions focused on the art of positive self-talk, mastering emotional waves, the science of manifestation, and skills that lift your vibration. Through the use of the written and spoken word you will enhance your wellbeing by integrating more positive thoughts, emotions and social aspects of life. The WAM (Words as Medicine) Program is a 10 week group or individual coaching program. Each week focuses on research-based skills to manage stress, increase self-awareness, improve emotional regulation, and deepen your understanding of how thoughts, emotions and behaviors are the key to a healthy, happy and easeful life. If you want to talk more about this process please click the start link below. Visit www.MichelleBee.com to learn more and schedule a free chat.

33 Days of Healing Words (Book)

Designed by a licensed therapist, these 33 bite-sized journal exercises are a simple, stimulating, and playful way to build healthy mental and emotional muscles. Each day of the healing journey is accompanied by a "let's do it together" video infused with high vibe music, affirmations, and guided journal prompts designed to help you succeed! These 33 guided journal prompts keep you thinking and reflecting on the positive for 33 days straight – giving support, inspiration and encouragement as you train yourself to focus on health and wellness. It takes 3-5 minutes a day, and it's perfect for beginner and seasoned journalers.

Searching for SHE (book)

In the poet-tree of life, Searching for SHE (Soul's Highest Expression) Poet and therapist Michelle Bee takes you on a journey from struggle to surrender. Searching for SHE (Souls Highest Expression), offers an inside look at the poetic process as a tool for transmuting anger, worry, doubt, and fear into LOVE. This book explores human obstacles that block the natural flow of love.

SHE is love. Love is all there is.

Claim your free 30-minute chat now to identify ways to create greater flow in your professional and personal life.

www.MichelleBee.com

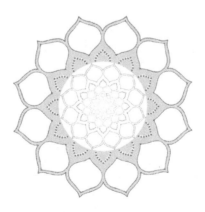

The End of Becoming
Radcliffe Johnson

I think we tried to get back home in our lives, we spent our entire life trying to get back to where we were when we felt safe the first time. Along the way, we get lost, until we find ourselves again through the journey. We lose the safety, the coverage, and we have to become that for somebody else to remember the feeling and then again for ourselves. The writings I've chosen for this chapter have built that place I call home.

I've made it my mission in life give meaning to my insights and experiences. This collection is part of my mission. Through poetry, I have discovered the clearest forms of expression. I don't know exactly what I'm going to say, I never know where my words come from, or how they're going to land... but it keeps landing me in a place that moves me forward. That forward movement has had a grounding impact on my life. The feedback from my own writing is a growth tool for enhancing life experiences. It comes from a place beyond, inside of me. It takes quiet, meditative practice to get access to that space beyond the conscious mind and that state of being is somebody I longed to become and in writing I become more and more of that person.

I met Steph at a transformative retreat years ago, where we took on breakthroughs and challenging tasks, such as walking on fire, board breaking, and other physical challenges. The conversations we shared about writing and publishing books in that context and environment imprinted on me a memorable experience that never rested nor subsided the possibility of becoming an author. Her confidence and competence resonated within me as we increased the risks and challenges of that day's events. That insight remained ever present and intriguing for many years as I built up my portfolio of poems determined to live a life of inspiration and growth worthy of publication. ~ Radcliffe

Radcliffe Johnson is a poet writing a conscious conversation about missed cues on the path of awareness. The son of Jamaican immigrants he was born in May Penne, Clarendon, Jamaica West Indies, visited the USA at age 8 and finally moved to Brooklyn New York, at age 11. His high school English teachers recognized his talents for expression and his stylistic approach to writing. He later revisited the missed cues from his youth and began writing poetry to his first love at age 23.

He now resides in California working on a poetry book, *A Year of Moments: A Collection of 365 Poems.* You can find his first book, Magical Creatures, on Amazon.

He sees emotions as mysterious cues to what's happening in the moment, to be expressed, experienced, observed, and constantly explored. If you would like to connect with Radcliffe, he invites you to join his Facebook group: www.facebook.com/groups/radcliffe.

Almost Home

I'm on my way home, so let me be.
I'm tired and I haven't much sleep, so please don't bother me.
I know you see me struggling, but let me be.
I may seem distant and so it shall be.
The man I need to be is waiting for me,
in a place I've never been, inside of me.

I have many miles to go,
the end I don't see.
I know you can help,
that I don't need.

I would love to share this walk with you,
but I won't speak,
a word of interest to anyone but me.

I believe you make great company,
but I won't be,
as a good listener as you may need me to be.

I need to do this alone, I do believe,
so please try to forgive
 or maybe put yourself in place of a man like me,
who belongs nowhere indeed.

Whenever I get there, I will be at peace.
I have never been there, but wait and see.
I will know it's home for there will be
no one there to welcome me
to the place where none have been before.
I am almost home.

Alone in the Dark

Alone in the dark
with my head on my pillow.
I have conversations with my witnesses
about their judgements of me.

The questions of the ones who watches me
through my own eyes,
who hears my thoughts,
observe me bargaining with them
until I choose.

Who I am, they know!

My keepers protect my inner being,
they know all that's happening with me.

They pull me back together,
whenever I fall apart.

They feel my fears,
they know my shame.

They are a committee of conversations
forming my character,
deciding who will represent our host in the moment.

The questions my witnesses ask of me
guide me through life
so, that I can become true to myself.

Destiny and Discipline

Every man has greatness in him
Through discipline he manifests himself.

What manner of man are you?
Do you hear the calling of your heart?
Do you believe in destiny?

To follow a path made only for you!
Do you dare to thread new roads?
Have all your dreams been dreamt for you?

To have no right, but to serve and fear the masters.
Dare disapproval!
Deny reassurance!

It is right to be weak and afraid!
Courage ascends of weakness and fear.
The chorus nest of fears!
Weaknesses conforms
In the maestro's choir harmony
Always looking left and right, to find your tune.

Does the frustration have you bored yet?
Do you know who you are?
Or that there is no you to know!

Does anyone know anything?
Do you know why you believe what you believe?
Are you willing to brave your choir's disapproval and break the
legacy?
Inspire, create and take distinct action.

We are pioneers, walking off roads without maps.
I am truly lost.
But I am free, and original!

Ego Within

We are always coming from a place within.

Hidden and guarded by our worst demons,

That which we are

Is unknown,

even to us who conceal it.

Buried and burrowed in the blind spot of our consciousness

Yet we are controlled by this puppet master

who pulls our strings,

and frames our motives.

The moment It is revealed to the light

it burrows deeper and escaping to a new hiding place

Within the awareness.

The perpetual game of

Self-discovery in a maze.

Humiliation

I am disgusted and humiliated with myself
Twisting and turning inside out
Unable to sleep at night.

Trying to figure out what I'm doing wrong.
I lost who I am
Chasing someone who clearly
does not want me.
I know I am being rejected.

I'm in Denial and I know it,
Yet, I want to hear those words.
I feel like I deserve a straight forward answer
But you're not going to be honest with me.

You'll continue to withhold and sabotage
The relationship with empty gestures,
Excuses and long delayed responses
To my messages until
I get frustrated and give up.

I'm being played;
Used.

I am pathetic and desperately in lust,
needing you while you rejected me
a long time ago.
I cowed when I should have left
with my dignity and self-respect intact.

I Wish that I Could Cry

No stormy clouds in my sky today,
Forecast: no rain.
Riverbeds and a dried salt trail.
Rage and wrath guard the dams upstream,
I have control.

The criminals love and pain can no longer touch my heart
and cause the rain to bleed.
The old guards know the culprits too well
They are quick and witty and well-rehearsed
To attack the villains approaching my walls.
-
Invaders die of thirst at my door
begging for a drop of tears
To fall from my cheeks.
Across the shrubs and rugged cheeks,
A salted desert greets all consort's tenderness.

I wish I could feel again
And it was possible to hurt my feelings.
To need someone.
To feel emotions.

The things I considered weak have abandoned me,
separating me from me.
Leaving this longing to feel the feelings
that caused the rain.

I've lost my humanity
Now that I am invincible and free,
from the vulnerability that really mattered to me.

I Wonder Where my Words Come From?

I wonder where my words come from?
Lying in bed, staring into the darkness,
I have no being that can be described.

There is no me that is in the past, only the void of awareness.

When I stop trying, I have no feeling.
When I stop thinking, I have no memory.

Where do my words come from?
I cannot see them until I've spoken them,
Then I am surprised that I made them real.

The moment I start to speak, it all comes back to me.
The moment I start to move I am me again.

Where does my movement come from?
I have no plan for where my feet land,
Yet when I walk, I take each step with certainty.

I can stand in the dark and not fall down,
Though I do not see where my feet meet the ground,
I am alive, and I did not plan it.
I will live, though I cannot say I want to.

Perhaps, I long to die and return to the void of conscientious.
The place I was when I asked the first question?
I wonder where my words come from?

In the End

I don't want to pay
for someone else's crime,
I'm an innocent man,
At least of this crime I stand accused.

Is there bad within my nature?
...bound to a life of crime?
Petty crimes to say the least,
Nothing illegal,
But small accumulations of injuries
That will over time break a heart.

Is that not the biggest crime of them all?
So, I am guilty after all
And the punishment saved me from
My inherent faults.

Incarnations

Through the stormy night
of violent forces,
I find my way in peril
forging stronger wings.

Soaring the heights
Beyond the breathable air of high
Altitude where colors fade
Into blacken skies and the stars
Begin to open their eyes.

A Quiet place where no sound can travel.
The sun at your back,
The Earth below,
Escaping gravity
with velocity into the expanse of the galaxy.

Loneliness

Great friend of mine,
We shared that bottle of wine
And so many delicious meals.

We watched movies
And listened to music
And shared indulgences that a glutton can appreciate.

I first met you when I was a child
Left alone in a quiet place
With only my cries to keep me.
I found you were my own voice
Echoing back at me in the emptiness of the dark.

We were introduced as strangers in the night.

There are times I see you in the crowd,
In a friend and sometimes a lover
You make me feel so good, to hurt so bad.

And everyone knows who you are,
Many avoid you; some cherish you.
I appreciate you
Loneliness.

Lost Souls

...and there are bodies
wandering about the nowhere.

The nowhere is the lost souls' somewhere.

These souls are the tears of the remnants
of living nightmares.

They are the haunted people,
warm bodies and cold souls.

Trapped among the living,
they linger in the communities of disorder
amongst disasters of people.

The survivors of the escapees,
that barely got away;
'Live to Tellers'

Tales of close calls and long gone,
Has-beens.
Schemers begging for favors,
humming the tunes of the hard-time blues.

Wagering against life;
the comfort zone of suffering for no reason;
where ignorance, fear
and conspiracies of the apocalyptic thrive.

Survivors undecisive about wanting to live,
they exist in a state of denial
as victims of their current,
past and future circumstances;
collaborators in their own misery.

They revisit their memories
of the highs, lows and in-betweens
In delirious laughing revivals.

Life does not exist in their eyes
rolled backwards into their skulls
relishing the delusional past,
seeing no hope forward,
craving for destruction and pain in the world.

They nourish themselves
on the thrills of reckless behaviors.

Forced into the tranquil life,
seemingly at peace,
these broken-hearted spirits are mended together by trauma.

Past Presents

To honor my past, I must go on

And live once more

And love once more

And be loved once more

I haven't dreamt a dream for so long

About loving a girl.

Soul Mate

I fell in love as I drowned in you,
The old me died as the pain of eternal loneliness evaporated
Of overwhelming pleasures kissing and making love to you,
The harmonics of two souls dancing on clouds
Seduced my will into surrender.

I found home when I was with you
I wanted no one else, nothing more
But to die for you,
Share all my days with you and die with you.

I dreamt of you when I was away
And wanted more time when we parted.

I always expected you to be in my life
I was infected by you,
Possessed by you, a haunting possession.

I never saw the end coming,
And how fast did my breaking heart get overpowered
By the pain inflicted upon me by your absence.

That death I said I was willing to suffer
Was not as I imagined.
To be torture like this, tormented by my own heart
For reasons that escapes me to this day.

And I have suffered year upon years,
Endless hell by the demons of my promises and hopes.

Yet I am alive,
Living an un-extraordinary life without you.
Those days of thunder and lightning
Are my better, in the past.

A stray smile sneaks upon my cheeks as a memory
Infects my mind and drags me into the mindscape
Of despair and gloom.

And I did fall in love again and again
There are many soul mates
Everyone I love, I love forever,
And never trespass onto the love of the others
And I failed them all
because I would not forget you,
And let you go.

I searched their motives to find your reasons.
I blamed them for the pain I carried for you.
I denied them the trust I lost to you.

I lived to protect myself
From what happened with you
And I lost them all.

But you remain my greatest and constant companion,
My mirror to reflect on all the wrongs I do.
That loss is a permanent scar upon my burnt face.
The mirror highlights my scar whenever I look at myself.

I hate myself, the fool I am,
I curse him daily.
I hate this pain I love so much,
Of always remembering you.

I hate the me that lost you.
I hate his pride, his vengeful pride,
His arrogance that told him he could live without you.

I met someone
She is my second chance at love,
My third second chance or perhaps my fourth.

I need to release you and let you live your life and I mine.
You moved on more eagerly than I did
And I resented you for that.

But I think you know how to win life.
And that, I will learn from you once again.

Love does not fall into righteousness.
Love is not about justice or goodness or fair dealings.
Love falls where love finds gravity's pull into orbit.
Love is the creator of dreams
And the destroyer of worlds.

Respect love, she is the master of all life.

I will forgive myself.
I will trust her.
I will not speak of you.
I will let her charms sway me into foolish promises.

I will forgive you through her and give away the kisses
I have withheld.
I will let my joyful heart have its chance to run free and
Be someone's soul mate once more.

I thank you my immortally beloved
As I set you free.

Goodbye.

Powerful

When I say the word Powerful
I am instantly intimidated by its implications.
Power is a demanding word,
Once spoken, merits a following of actions.
Can I deliver on my declaration to be Powerful?

Fear emerges, justifying my reasons why I will fail.
The comforts of mediocrity are a safe haven
I've acclimated myself to.

Dare not dream too big.
Dare not express what's real.
Dare not risk the unknown.

I choose to be Powerful and be seen.
I Choose to give all and be expressed
I Choose to dream the impossible dream,
Chest striking upward.
Courage and love are my armor.

Venturing into the darkness and the light.
Welcome to the world, unknown.
I stand vulnerable and open to account for my life
Before all of mankind.

I feel the flow of time passing through me.
Powerfully delivering into the world a distinct being...

I am accepting into myself all of you before me.
Seeing you, Love.
I give you, Love.
You are powerful!
I am free, an eternally powerful being.

RAGE

There is a monster
beyond the reach of the conscious mind.
A demon buried within each of us.

RAGE!

Its primal fierceness unleashes uncontrollable violent.
its emergence is sudden,
it acts quickly,
sharply and brutally,
violence in peak form.

Destroying whatever is in its path;
A starving beast feast,
ripping apart human flesh with gleeful satisfaction,
to an end of murder!

This demon exists for a reason
and when summoned,
death occurs.

She Loves Him Too

All those days spent together,
Long looks, sweet kisses and endless laughter.

Dreaming about the next advances.
First the looks that clears the kiss.
To roaming hands and exploring curiosities.

A solvent puzzle has no charms.

Two quiet repentant lovers torn apart.
As too many words from a wounded heart
Creates the rise for a new start.

And now that reality must be acknowledged.
She finds another fantasy to begin again.

While your dreams are dying
her possibilities are expanding.

And yes, she loves him too as she loved you.
His eyes offer the spark you lost.
His kisses are fresh and has no bitter taste.

Nothing between them but love.

The frailty of passion has no room for pain.

Only lust can claim a place at the table that has no shame.

Sway

Indifferent stature of loneliness
Daunting with splendor, striding seclusion
Sway, sway bountiful woman of sovereign estate
Who are you?

Woe and descend thy mighty thrown
Oh vaulted heart, open thy doors
Give life a chance to deliver you home
Wash pride away, allow tears to flow

Fly high O' wingless bird
Dream the clouds a solid floor
Smile, your heart has found its home
Be renewed,
a dreaming boy's fancy once more.

Sweet Surrender

The surrender of your body
Reassuringly falling into my arms.
Closer and closer the press of our hips.
The deepest kiss of unbroken lips.

searching finger tips
gliding against the heat of skin
Closing our eyes as we both fall
Into sweet surrender of a lover's arms.

Two bodies synced in single harmony
eyes affixed in mirrors smiling.
Life springs out of the moment's bliss
Making love the eternal kiss.

Swimming

With you I pledge this sacred vow, marrying you my one true love.
Swimming in the currents of loves endless ocean.

This blissful joy lightens my feet, my heart is free,
Where I have found my home in true companionship.

And all the satisfying works of maintaining my secret paradise
Rewards me with your smile beneath those glowing eyes
Emitting the radiance of loves most beautiful shine.

And yes, we are busy people working for tomorrow's benefit.
Looking up from my task and seeing my beloved smiling back at
me.

I surrender to my fate in your arms.
Celebrating every day with you as a blessing gifted to me as life's
highest honor.

And when the fading sun sets in your eyes, as I, in my wanderlust
drift off in your warm gaze towards adventure; satisfying my soul.

I know my heart has found its home, and all my dreams became
true
In the mundane activities of daily life, when my thoughts guide my
actions
In consideration of your wellbeing,
These unwavering kindnesses and good intentions fulfill our
destiny as Husband and Wife.

The End of Becoming

In the end
I will land at my destination
Whole and intact,
A complete human being.

The path that led me home
Tested my soul.

Through trials and tribulations
I endured the unsettling feelings tormenting my soul.

All the anxieties of the unknown
Became my comfort zone.

I no longer feared the unknown
But rather seek to make friends
On those unexplored roads.

Peace became my home
Knowing that wherever I am,
I am always there with other human souls.

The Fog

Is it right to be lost and have no way out of this fog in my head?

My family need me to be strong.
I am afraid to be weak and need someone.
though my words are grand,
They are empty of what matters In who I am.

I want to show them all my value
and yet every attempt leaves me more and more alone
in this fog.

I don't want to be wrong,
for what I have done to others when they were,
I fear will be done to me.
and such a mirror have lie to me my whole life
and I knew all along to look behind the curtains.

This act of living to be perfect
catches up to me at night when I am alone
with my demons by my side,
I triumph before the sun rise
and garb my facade out the door.

I am a man and I do not know how to be one.
I live out of routines and affectations.

Running a race against opponents in my head telling me who I am.
Never letting my heart feel its fair share of life's burdens.

Using my heart after so lazy a life,
I want to protect it and hide the bruises I endured,
so, no one can see me as who I always feared I was.

The Lost Moments I Wait for

I think about you all the time.

All day I wait for the moment I am with you

To be greeted by smiling lips, ear to ear

Long gazes that erase my mind

Gentle touch to surrender and melt

I feel no fear when I'm with you

Though, I should be terrified

That someone might see us

And know that we are more than just friends

I don't want to give you up to be right.

So, I'll hide and betray my world

Because, you exist.

The Finest Hour

Alchemy has borne fruit,

A golden flower,

Drenched of passion's awesome power,

A fury awakening by this hour

A glorious moment I devour,

To touch a star in silence.

The sound of silence

The chaos embedded within
the sounds of nothingness
forms an image in my mind's eye
of the vast voided emptiness
in the darkness behind the closed eyes abyss
of terrifying descent.

The quietness echoes the anxiety
of the listening inquisitor
Asking the void "am I alone in here?"

Watching the conversation between the listeners and the
questioners.
as I witness fear itself summon the darkest of sounds.

I am not alone in the dark.
I know there are my many selves in here
and they frightened each other most of all.

In the light I pretend I am alone
But in the darkness,
 I know I am not.

The Missing Words

When silence goes on too long,
there is a message communicated.

A heart that speaks its truth also listens,
and when there is too much silence,
Suspicion and doubt hear
their worries confirmed.

The same anxiety gap
exists in the other's heart,
synchronizing two lovers.

They know their pace and rhythm
and when one heart
sends out its affection to the other,
absence of reciprocation,
the seeds of suspicion interpret
the anxieties as abandonment and betrayal.

The search begins for the exit doors.
The eyes no long lock and hold.
The heartbeats rest.
Passions cool.

The others touch is cold
and terrifying.
Loneliness returns home
because someone forgot to lock the doors.

The Music Safe

She walks in,

Like the cold morning air invading a warm house.

Striding on quiet light and colorful sounds,

Into the desperate void of jealous eyes.

Falling into a vacuum beneath my feet,

My words and emotions

Are weighted to the ground

too heavy to traverse the room.

Watching them falling into a hole beneath my chin,

Like autumn leaves riding a mild breeze to the ground.

A supernatural presence permeates the occasion,

My Heart is reverberating like a pounding drum in the abyss of my body.

The heat, is a hot cup of tea brewing within a lost consciousness

Grasping for air below the waterline,

Drowning in wine.

Her voice modulated a melody,

Like wings on each syllable.

A little extra something, here and there,

Every word exuding a piece of her soul.

I am feasting on her loveliness

captured by beauty

Animated in the life of a muse.

Impossibly beautiful,

Yet strangely perfect that I would have missed her,

Had I not taken the chance and looked twice.

Into eyes darker than night, but bright,

Brighter than the rising sun over the mountains.

And listen to the voice of love accentuated in her tongue.

The moment we touched,

And embrace,

she smiles,

 surrendering and closing

Her honest eyes

fading and disappearing

Back into the box that kept her

Music safe.

The Orbit

We are orbiting like two black holes spinning out of control,
intoxicated with this high, destined to collide.

Yearning for you to touch me again
And feel those cold tiny fingers melting on my hot skin,
And breathe your scent into my mouth, so I can taste you.

I want to kiss those tiny lips and taste your smile.
Your words seem so delicious coming off those curling lips.

I see you watching me, watching you,
pleading to feel the crawl of your warmth fused with mine.

I want you to infect my heart with your venom
And drown my thoughts in your wonder.
Silencing this seeping hunger,
Awakening the demon's appetite.

All these words aren't wasted between us,
For we are not talking,
We are fornicating through our conversation
Looking for a reason to meet in bed
And exorcised this possession.

The Painting

I like seeing my reflection in your eyes,
wondering what you see in me.

A frame of time,
a moment of permanence.
You look at me every day
and see a difference.
I can't change,
but you do.

I worry when you don't look at me
as If you've lost interest.

I like it when you come back to me
after long times of walking by
without a hello
or a goodbye,
and look at me with new eyes
full of life and curiosity about me again.

Those days are my best days,
when it seems like you love me again
like when we were both young
and new to each other.

Transition

Waking up today and realizing I slept alone last night,
You're not there,
The house is eerily quiet.

I'm waiting for the sounds
Of your key turning in the door as you come home,
Your voice calling me with certainty.

I want to answer the echoes in my mind with words
But I'm hallucinating
Your laughter as you found my surprise gifts
on the kitchen table next to the flowers that I never let die.

I always brought you flowers and things that kept your beauty
shining through.

Now I have nothing to look forward to in my day.

You are gone.
I am saddened;
dazed by the surprise of how we parted.

How is it the woman I love does not love me anymore.

When did I miss the clues?

I am in transition,

From a dream back into reality
and reality hurts,
it hurts all the time.

To touch you was my highest privilege and joy.
And now I have nothing to look forward to
 in these endless days,
as I look at the door
that your key to the lock on my heart
will never turn again.

The Ecology of Ghettoes

The first step towards my current destination

Began with an abrupt end to my childhood

My exposure to the unsheltered life of neglect.

The guidance and security of adults disappeared in the streets of the ghetto.

My skin crawled raw within the threatening atmosphere feeling desperation preying on weaknesses.

A crucible boiling a soup of poisonous creatures stirred by the political puppet masters.

Everyone struggled to escape the harvesting of the apex predators;

who comfortably reigned over the concrete jungle.

The rangers and medics cleaned up in the morning, counting the corpses and aiding survivors.

Holding no one accountable for the reckless indulgences of the hunters in the dark.

The Vultures scavenging the streets kept their bellies filled with the abundant spillage of loose cubs wandering the streets unattended all hours of the days and nights.

The traps laid by wolves,

The lions patrolled the boulevards,

The hyenas laughing on street corners

Boastfully jay-walking out into to traffic

to hustle up a meal.

The prey barely ate,

They felt secure within their ever-increasing numbers sprawling the wall-less prison.

The tension brewed courage and sharpened cunning.

The survival instincts edged a thrilling adventure into daily life.

Playing with fire burned nerve endings and desensitized the nervous system to dangerous circumstances.

The prey got comfortable being hunted

Knowing more people cared if they were dead than alive.

Those who viewed us as unworthy cried whenever we escaped into the safety of their neighborhoods.

The Wait

The weight of anticipation slows time
In the depth of the silence between the two sides of this
conversation
I've been waiting for all my life.

What pressing matter has her ignoring me?

Does she not know that everything in
my world must stop until I hear her words?

I will not retreat from my gifts of praise and unconditionality,
Though the fires of rejection are burning at my feet.
I stand in the flames with arms and heart wide open.

No retreat!

I will not rethread this course.
I feel the fears and hurts in the chasm of silence.

We were friends and now that this bridge must be crossed;
You may abandon me,
For the course I am on does not hear considerations.

There is but one way and that is forward,
Into the pain and the den of hungry lions.

What must be said is usually between lovers.

Rarely does a friendship survive this weather.

Will you choose to shelter me beneath your umbrella,
or shall we dance in the rain together?

This bridge I must cross among many others are on my path
home,
Between here and forever.

Love

I long to hear the comfort of a heartbeat in her chest.

While feeling the warm touch of love comforting me.

I miss the kisses that held too long and eyes that do not blink in locked gazes.

Voices that invite trust and kindness.

Whisper of 'I love you' while I sleep in peace and feel her voice seeping pleasant lullabies into my heart.

And when my eyes open
to see you in the morning bright,
my dream begins again.

Solitude

In solitude of this quiet mind

I find the time to explore infinity.

To look around the perimeters of forever and survey my life spent on wasted worries.

In gratitude I appreciate those lost years

And pay a tribute with a flood of tears.

And all those wondering days spent lost,

Not knowing how to get to where I stand today.

That loneliness which kept my hunger unsatisfied and yearning for more than comfort and ease.

How thankful I am for that beautiful suffering in moments that unsettled me.

How grateful I am for this life,

I existed and witnessed

I live to tell of my journey and contribute to the success of the human enterprise,

however far we may go into the infinite unknown.

Realms

The awakened ones walking among us
Have inner kingdoms of peaceful treasure.

Their walls are dignified and tall
Built slowly through time
to hold under the siege of plunder.

Manned by the refined senses of deep insight and astute
intelligence.

Guarded by a sharp-witted minds and good judgment.

The toll of admission is but an honest soul.
Paying with peace and carrying the torch of truth.

The entrance lies within the strangers' eyes,
behind the door guarded by the human soul,
Who knows a kindred spirit looking for a place
we all remember as home.

The Inconvenience of the Talented

The inconvenience of the talented is an eruption disturbing the human soul.

The driving impulse to explore the realms of suffering in search of art.

A journey through the unpleasant depths of loneliness,

an artists must endure in extracting art from the realm beyond the boundaries of the conscious mind.

The suffering is priced equivalent to the magnitude of one's creation.

The artist imposes a cost onto himself.

Everyday life is in the way,

Circumstances conspire against you.

Inconveniences compound themselves

And Life becomes difficult to live

without art being interwoven into the substance that affirms existence.

The work of living this particular life

demands commitment to a standard

of integrity and honesty

that permits the inner vision

to see truths that resonate

with those who thirst to live a purposeful life.

The artist ingests the raw materials of life,

And give birth to artistic expression.

The artist cannot exist

without the ever-present unease consuming his peace,

pressing him in discontentment with comfortable escapism.

Driven by these intense passions to extreme and abrupt life changes.

In solitude he finds the harmony between himself and his art.

His soul transmutes his labors into beautiful majestic art.

The Forgotten One

Tell myself I am not forgotten.
Though Your silence is an estimation
of my value to you.
I needed the closure of the word goodbye.

Am I forgotten or do you resent me?

I prefer to be resented than forgotten.
At least you are thinking of me
I am not irrelevant
I made some different to you.

You missed me!

To be forgotten erases me from existence
These memories are illusions,
phantom feelings in a feedback loop
within myself.

It hurts to know I am delusional
And all that I did was for nothing.

I sold my heart lies and it believed me,
dreamt a future that will never be.

I gave myself away to an empty gesture.

The shame of the fool I am
Breaks my heart and humiliates me
in my own eyes.

I don't want to tell anyone
The truth,
Now that I know I am nothing to you.

The dismissal of being ignored
Drains my enthusiasm for living.
Yes, I am forgotten,
nothing I was ever mattered to you
And now I fade into the abyss of obscurity.

Leviathans

There are those rare few;
Individuals who are astonishing human beings;
Truly extraordinary people.
People who inspire you by who they are.
When one of them touches your life,
you are transformed.
Like a Phoenix riding the flame from the ashes
ascending into the night sky,
birthing a midnight sun.

A new you emerge,
unable to return to the pain
and lethargy of mediocrity.

Your body becomes more vigorous and vibrant.
You feel life's energies
flowing throughout your body
for the first time,
as urgency and opportunity.

The awaken mind has a vision.
The touched heart pumps love
and gratitude into the world.

You become the source of creation.
You act responsibly.
You change from what you can get out of life
and become about what you can give in life.

Your actions serve the lives of others.
You are fulfilled by watching them thrive,
As you begin to see how your impact can echo into eternity.

Things that are beautiful

When I think of you,

I escape my body,

My circumstances,

My troubles.

My whole world disappears

And I am floating in ecstasy.

The fountain of rejuvenation

Flows over my shoulders

Washing away my tension and stress.

My mind gets a refreshing injection of inspiration and ideas.

My boundaries expand to a new frontier

Of human experience,

As I smile at the thought

That you provide so much fulfillment

In my life simply by your presence in it.

Father

Father, watching you, I see the man I want to be.
You are everything I've ever needed.

When I hurt, your comforting washes away my pain.
Through you I learned to trust.

I know you will always catch me.

When you lifted, I fly,
I became a plane and flew the sky.

I closed my eyes, flew among the birds,
I soared the open skies without fear of heights
Because I had my navigator at my side.

Your warm gentle touch comforts me,
I am not afraid.

I am loved, of that, I am sure.

I will not fear in my father's grasp.
I know you love me so,
I am brave when I see you watching as I try.

I may fall so many times; I will rise as many times.
I know that when I lose,

I'm still winning it for you.
I earn the biggest prizes in your praises and your cheers.

You're proud of me, I know.

I am strong in my father's eyes.

You teach me to be kind.

I feel and know secure.

My father's love is pure.

I know you will endure whatever it may take
To keep our house a home for me to dream at night
Of being just like you.

Dark Waters

The river came to town one morning
And the mountains seemed so small as they stood
With their heads peeking above dark waters.

The forever land disappeared as trees
And hills breathe through straws.

Terror and fear ruled the land
as rooftops covered with dogs
the birds all drowned,
the emptied skies quieted the wilderness
and brought about the end of the world.

People became frightened, silent and kind,
Feuding clans stood side by side
Staring in disorientation,
Inches away from a fascinating death
Ferociously streaming through paths,
men only a few days earlier they walked.

The waters made thunder and rolled into beautiful braids.

The Gray luminescent skies ate the Stars, the Moon and Sun;
And when the lightning came, we knew it was Judgment Day.

No one slept that night,

We ate crackers and sipped hot chocolate
Listening to the sounds
Of rain striking the zinc roofs like bullets.

The rain flew uphill,
The howling wind toppled trees,
They wailed as loudly as the goats and cows
When their branches were torn away.

All the worms ran away
And became surface dwelling sky watchers.
Worry filled the atmosphere,
We knew the people that live where
The endless dark waters now strolled
And they were not there anymore.

Nothing was the same anymore!

The Dawn Comes

The burning red skies on the horizon announces the beginning.

The flames beneath the clouds stealing away the darkness,
As the stars begin closing their eyes.

Awe has taken captives,
The dawn is here!

A speckle of light growing ever brighter
Seeping over the mountain's ridge.

The whole valley turns to see the ascending eye,
A seamless wonder embarks, reigning the dawn onto land.

Brightness streaming from the core.

The charging barrage of stifling light
Erupting out from the ascending star.

My heart is full and satisfied.

The shroud of darkness receding likes waves,
In the grafting between the two worlds.

The emerging day now approaches the earth's stage,
As the retreating night's beauty moves on.

The falling star

The strong man enjoys his thrown
With all the praises, his happiness grows;
But we know too well how this goes.

We wait in anticipation for the slip of his toes,
When the weight of his hubris tips his thrown.

The lights are flashing as he falls to the floor.

And hungry audience celebrate his throes
And contribute by tossing in all of their stones,
Stored over time in patience and spite,
The vigor of passions explodes and ignites.

When reprisal come knocking at a falling man's door.

Does he know his sins and accept what he owes?

A Love Letter to Trauma, Thank You for the Life I Live

Steph Ritz

This is a true story of how life-altering terrifying moments led me to find safety in creativity, revealed my life purpose, and how trauma led me to explore the gifts that make up everything I do today.

It's with deep gratitude that facing gut-wrenching fear and life-threatening danger changed my path in life forever.

This is a story about the 12 months between being evaluated for Reading Special Education and becoming an award-winning performer, published author, and book editor... at the age of 12.

Can I just say... these twelve months you're about to hear about were some of the most pivotal of my life – foundational experiences setting patterns that would completely alter the course of how others would see me, and how I saw myself.

The River Goddess

I still remember my first recurring dream. We moved when I was three years old, and at the new house I started to have the same dream, over and over. I started dreaming of a woman in a canoe, coming up the river that flowed through my backyard, gliding magically upstream, passing my house on the way to my neighbors' backyard. She wore a thin summer white linen dress and was crowned with the most magnificent wreath of flowers blossoming with the profusion of the season's bounty, with thin silk ribbons with scalloped edges in pastels trailed in tendrils above her wild tangle of tender blonde curls. It was such a wonderful dream.

I kept dreaming of the river goddess on her way to my neighbors, so I went to my neighbor Toni to tell her about my dream. I think it was the first time I saw someone ugly cry. I didn't know what to do, she was sobbing so hard. I went and sat at her feet, put my hand on her knee, patted it a bit. At some point, my neighbor's crying calmed, we switched to where Toni was patting my hand on her leg, and she kept nodding and swallowing. I could tell she wanted to say something, but the words seemed stuck in her throat.

She gestured for me to wait and went to another room in her house. I waited what felt like forever, but I could hear her rummaging. My neighbor returned with a photo album. And wouldn't you know it... there was The River Goddess in all her glory; it was the same person from my dream!

It took Toni a couple tries, her words hitching, her breath catching, her resolve resettling, before she could tell me my River Goddess was her mother who had passed away not long before I became her neighbor. I dreamed that dream so many times while I lived in that house; it always washed me in an ethereal calm.

Early Years

When I was in first grade, my twin and I were both put into the advanced class in a tracked system. But we could not be in the same classroom, did not get along even at that age. He stayed in the advanced group, and I was moved down to the basic class.

Even at 6 years old, I was well-aware I'd been downgraded. In a tracked system, switching classes meant moving from reading with classmates to a class learning sight words. As a stubborn, scorned child, I stupidly decided to stop reading. I felt they were calling me dumb. Why I decided to prove them right I'll never understand.

My eyes absorbed everything, but my mouth no longer opened – it no longer felt safe to share what I knew or didn't know.

By the end of first grade, I'd forgotten most of what my mom had worked so determinedly to teach us, erasing the leg-up privilege she had bought with her marriage to my mentally ill millionaire father.

A year later, my second-grade teacher took pity on me and bribed me – I relearned what I'd lost during after school lessons while enjoying my teacher's homemade chocolate-molded lollipops.

Even though I could read, I still didn't feel safe letting others know what I knew, and by 5th grade, I landed in testing for Reading Special Education. Hand me a dry, boring, crappy, white-washed biased curriculum book, and I could barely make it through one paragraph. Put a compelling book in front of me and I could read for hours... but I wasn't letting anyone know.

I'd been picking random bubbles on the scantron tests - I wouldn't even read the questions before using the ABCDE columns to create pictures and patterns with the filled in bubbles.

Once a week, for all of one month, I went to a reading specialist. Didn't take her long to figure out I could read just fine when I felt like it, and that my comprehension was years ahead of my age.

Solitude

It shouldn't be surprising to hear I started summer break grounded to my room. After the shenanigans I'd pulled during the school year, it was to be expected. Being grounded was quite normal in my house, it was the most common tactic my parents used. Tuck that child out of sight, insist on silence and isolation, and make 'em write an essay to get out of "jail". No screens, no games, no toys. No time outside the bedroom except for meals or bathroom break… and then I better walk quietly enough not to raise the wrath of my father.

I was still grounded over a month later. Refused to write an essay explaining why I was wrong. Bored out of my mind doesn't begin to describe the miserableness of endless days by myself.

Directly across from my open bedroom door I could see my older sister's bookshelf. I stood there staring at all those books, each so different from one another. I'd been locked in my room for a month already. There was nothing else for me to do, and she was away at summer camp. I was lonely, bored, and feeling equally helpless, restless, and resentful.

While I can't remember the order I read those books, so many of the titles are still crystal clear in my mind's eye. Hardcover copies of *Heidi* and *Little Women* with goldleaf edges, a pocket-sized song book, a tattered copy of *Dune*, and a beautifully illustrated children's book of Lao Tzu's writings are some of the books I remember from that magical collection.

Perhaps the most life altering and influential book I read that summer was *Valley of the Horses* by Jean Auel.

Here I was reading a book that seemed to explain everything my mom passively instilled in me about her beliefs: love of outdoors, appreciation for Mother Earth, curiosity for the natural world, listening to instincts, connecting with wild animals, wilderness survival, the feel of flying on horseback and pounding across an open field, and so much more. That book illustrated the process of feeling held and shaped by the invisible hands of grace and goodness.

I had grown up in a house where religion was not discussed, but surely this is what Christians feel when they're holding the bible! Who knew a book could reveal so many ideologies and ideas! Here was a strong female protagonist, a true role model, isolated for years, who was not only finding ways to survive anything nature put in her path but was thriving in the harshest and extreme conditions.

How unbelievably lucky (and lovingly supported by Earth-Momma) was I to be introduced to sexuality through ceremonial ways to embrace losing my virginity, how to use the moon to predict my bleeding cycles, how to be (and not to be) touched by a lover, and the existential pain and pleasure that comes with crystal clarity clairvoyance.

That magical non-bible book written by an empowered and passionate female author cast so many stones skipping across the clean-slated surface of my youthful mind, creating lasting impressions that would ripple through my life for years to come.

Something about that book allowed my own ears to hear my soul's voice. It also allowed me to admit I had chosen a hurtful way to express my emotions. Who knew storytelling could create a safe container?

Witness

After months grounded to my room, I had gotten used to walking around silently and unseen for snacks and stretches. On one of my trips down to the kitchen, I came across my parents in a heated fight. My dad was mentally ill and we all generally avoided him - arguing was uncommon.

I don't know what made me move from my hiding spot in the formal dining room but I went to break up the fight. Something in me knew that my presence was just the reminder they needed to realize they were not alone, that there was a witness. I instinctively knew it would calm my father's tirade.

I got to the doorway just in time to see my dad chuck the lid of our tin container of marbles at my mom. He whirled at my gasp and left. I rushed to my mom's side. Even though the projectile was super lightweight, it left a mark where it ricocheted off her leg. A once-benign object had transformed into a weapon, and her welt was the same pink color as the flower decoration on the copper colored tin.

The shock of violence is always jarring, whether physical, mental, or emotional. I held her hand, saying nothing. What could a kid say to their parent in a post-abuse explosion? We were both crying – mine leaky like a drippy faucet with tears sliding down my face every time I blinked, while Mom was overcome with shoulder-shaking sobs rolling from her. She still sat where she'd been when my father had approached and attacked. We stayed like that for a long time, until her fear and grief had burned up the adrenaline released during the confrontation, eventually disbursing back into the universal pool of constantly recycled energy.

Freedom

My first taste of freedom in two months was a trip to see an abortion doctor. No, it wasn't like that. My mom went to see an abortion doctor about a job.

My parents can best be described as activist extremists – inspiring, sometimes scary, and always embroiled in passion and crisis. One of the big "causes" my family was involved with was women's rights. According to the pro-choice movement, I am a second-generation unicorn... a mythical magical creature who defies all boundaries of understanding. You see, my dad's life (and therefore mine too) only exist because of the pro-choice movement. Turns out his dad was sterile and my dad's mom participated in some of the very first artificial inseminations. Yep, my dad is a turkey baster baby. My life is literally the cross-point of the pro-choice pro-life argument, where both sides sit on the same side of the fence.

My parents would spend their days as escorts standing outside of abortion clinics. My dad, as a hobbyist photographer, began snapping hundreds of photos of "the anti's" doing illegal things to keep patients from getting into the clinic.

Up until that point in my life, neither of my parents had jobs (talk about privilege!). But my dad is the one who controlled the money. And my mom needed money for a divorce attorney.

After months of isolation, it wasn't all that hard for my mom to woo me to the abortion doctor's house with the promise of a lake party so she could schmooze the doctor for a job.

Swimsuits at the ready, Mom and I pulled into this giant estate. There were already least 20 other cars in the giant estate's driveway, and plenty of room to park another 20. Among all the Beamers, Benz's, and Audi's, our minivan looked ridiculously out of place. This was a party for the clinic workers, patient escorts, and other upper crust financial supporters of the Pro-Choice movement.

On her first jump off the short (not-proverbial) pier, Mom lost her prescription sunglasses in the lake. She gave up after a few minutes searching, completely embarrassed. With no other kids at this adult party, what else was I to do besides spend the next two hours trying another couple hundred times to find the glasses?

There was something so peaceful about skimming my fingers through the gentle fuzzy green weeds, diving down to the bottom, bubbles sliding up my swimsuit in a steady stream to the surface, toes touching air, stirring up the sandy silt with my searching hands.

Determination and motivation can be a pretty powerful duo. When Mom and I reconnected, we were both triumphant: me with the glasses, and her with a job offer.

On the way home I would learn this would be her first job since marrying my rich dad, She was a store clerk on food stamps with a toddler at home before marrying my trust-fund baby of a dad. Now, she would be a secretary job at the doctor's abortion clinic. She was, once again, doing whatever she could to build a safe future for her children.

The Wanderer

After that summer locked away daydreaming through book character's eyes, I started having other types of daydreams too.

If I slipped into an eye's-open mind-loose blank-canvas state of consciousness, I could teleport into someone else's experiences, seeing an outsider's viewpoint in limited perspective like watching a tv show filmed with one still camera.

I shared a daydream I'd had with my mom, and described walking beside her into her new divorce lawyer's office. I described colors, pictures, tons of vivid details that my mom verified as absolutely true.

I'm not sure my mom looked at me the same ever again.

Positioning of the Sacred Feminine

I had never seen the Milwaukee Art Museum lit up at night. A parking attendant waited for us as we pulled into the lot, and it seemed like every relative who lived in the state was there that night.

After an obligatory multi-generational photo for the local newspaper, we walked into the event to applause... I was confused why the artwork from my dad's mom's apartment was now hanging on the walls of the museum. The wall also had my last name printed on it! And there was a stack of books to match! She was donating all this art to the museum!

I remember Grandma Ritz making a speech about being Jewish activist yet collecting German art, art Hitler thought unworthy and often destroyed but would later become astronomically valuable historically, culturally, and financially.

Her catalogue was organized by phases of art, artists, and style, with historical notes and commentary, and a plate list cataloguing each piece's size and medium details.

The signature picture of *A Breadth of Vision: The Ritz Collection* mirrored a snapshot of my twin brother and me as toddlers. (Who buys a painting merely because it looks like a snapshot of their grandkids?!). Choosing the *Brothers* painting as the cover art of her collection was quite possibly the highest honor my Grandma Ritz could ever pay to my brother and me. Years later, when she passed away and I went for my second after-hours museum visit for her memorial, the only thing I asked to inherit was that silver framed snapshot of my brother and I that matched the *Brothers* painting.

Listening to the Divine Masculine

That year, I saw death for the first time when my mom's dad was in a coma at the end of his life, dying of the same colon cancer that killed all five of his brothers. We went to say goodbye to Grandpa and to be with Grandma as she went through the last few days of his at home hospice care.

Grandpa was a quiet man; most of my memories of him include being in the same space silently being present with a stillness that spread serene calmness to the chaos of five grandchildren underfoot. I could watch him for hours, happily basking in his stoic presence. Silently watching Grandpa do whatever chore he felt like doing was a lot better than having to help Grandma weed her garden... especially on manure spreading days.

On Grandpa's last day of life, my mom and grandma went to the grocery store together, and my brother went with them... which would leave me alone with comatose Grandpa.

When they left the house, I sat down on the carpet-scrap-covered hassock at the side of the couch. At first, I remember feeling uncomfortable, nervous. But I wasn't scared by the presence of my dying grandpa as much as I was afraid to speak and disturb him, I was more afraid not to speak and have him think he was all alone.

I remember slowly rubbing melting ice chips over his parched lips, and seeing the slightest turning of the head. Was he asking for more? Was he nuzzling my hand, cherishing contact? With my whole being, I knew he was aware. He knew I was there; he knew he wasn't alone.

As I sat at his side, I let my heart infuse my tongue with all the words I was afraid to speak. I remember telling him I loved him. I told him it was okay to go, but I also asked him to wait for Grandma to get back first. I reassured him the pain of this body would not follow him. I promised him we'd take care of Grandma. It was a very clear conversation, yet I don't remember if I actually spoke aloud. Still, I knew he heard me.

When everyone returned from their errands, my mom and us kids loaded up to go home, and left Grandma to usher Grandpa out of this world. We made it less than an hour away from their house before he took his last breath, though it'd be another couple of hours before we'd get word.

Dreamwalking

After sharing that silent conversation with my grandpa as he transitioned out of his body, I started stepping into the dreamer. I could look through the eyes of the dreamer, hear from their ears as if my body was superimposed over them. Or maybe it was more like being embedded into their being? How differently others perceived the world!

Whether at home or at sleepovers with friends, I'd inevitably dream someone else's dream. It was just a matter of time before I figured out whose dream I'd dreamed. Often, I could identify the dreamer based on our shared moods, feelings, emotions, desires, and passions during the dream.

These shared dreams are how I recognized I was in mortal danger the instant I saw light glint off the knife in my brothers hand...

The Chase

On a clear and cold winter Saturday night, my parents left town to attend an opera. My twin brother and I were both grounded to our rooms - as per usual. We were old enough to not need a babysitter and too young to be trusted alone, so our parents charged us with reporting on the other.

But not long after they'd left, I heard my brother watching tv downstairs in the living room so I decided to go over to my best friend's house a few doors down. He told me not to go, watching tv in the house alone wasn't the same thing as leaving in his eyes. I told him to do whatever he felt like doing and I was going to do what I wanted.

When I got home from visiting with my neighbor, my brother came at me with a butcher knife. It wasn't the first time he threatened me with knives... walking around menacingly with the tip pointed at me, or stabbing our solid wood butcher block hard enough to brake off blade tips had become regular intimidation tactics.

This time was different. I saw out-of-control fury. I was terrified. I ran to my room, with my twin brother chasing me with a 12-inch butcher knife. I slammed the door closed and braced myself against the door, knowing I was pursued. I was terrified.

The full body slam against the door was enough to pop it open, but I pushed back again with all my strength, my back flat against the dark oak door, shoes digging into the cream-colored carpet, both hands on the doorknob trying to keep him from turning the handle and unlatching it again. I managed to get the door closed again and again, fighting with every ounce of strength I could muster against the onslaught of him using his body as a battering ram. Then he started stabbing the door. Over and over again, he stabbed me in the back... with all of two inches of wood protecting my flesh from a fatal wound. That's when terrified turned to hysterical calm.

Eventually there was silence from the hallway. I didn't move from my position against the door, didn't let go of the knob. I knew my twin well, of course there was a second round of attack. The second attempt to break down my door and stab me was much shorter, followed by an eerie gut-sickening maniacal laugh that would haunt my dreams for decades. I heard his footsteps running down the stairs. Listening through the air vent, I heard the recliner chair squeaking open as he settled back in front of the TV.

I knew I had to leave. I couldn't protect myself. I was already exhausted.

I wrote a note to my mom about what had happened, and where I'd gone (back to the neighbor's four doors down). If he did end up killing me as I tried to flee the house, at least there'd be a record that it wasn't an accident.

But if he found the note, surely I'd be dead sooner rather than later, so I slipped it out of sight between my dresser and the wall.

My heart still pounding, I crept down the stairs and as quietly as possible snuck out the front door and ran.

I didn't know if my brother had heard me leave. I didn't know if he was pursuing me. If he was right behind me.

It was clearly past bedtime, but there was still a light on upstairs at the neighbors. I knew they had strict rules in their house but I didn't know where else I could go. I started knocking.

A light came on.

The door opened to the dad in flannel plaid pj's with worn down leather slippers looking highly agitated.

A fresh set of tears came on so fast, I remember barely being able to get words out to ask if I could stay there, constantly looking over my shoulder in fear to see if my brother was following. It was clear to the neighbor that something was wrong and that I didn't feel safe standing on the doorstep.

I remember him asking questions as he led me to the family room couch and handed me a box of tissues. There were more questions while he grabbed a pillow and a blanket. I agreed to go home as soon as I woke up, as my parents would be returning home to find my bed empty and no clue where I gone (pre-cellphone era).

The next morning, I could still feel the fear of the night before coursing through me. My senses felt overstimulated by the scent of coffee, the sound of the percolator popping, and cabinets and drawers opening and closing. It was the beginning of blue hour, the all-encompassing black melting into deep blues. I got up and went to the kitchen to find the dad. He told me he always got up first and would bring coffee to his wife in bed. He quietly let me out of his house so I could sneak back into my own bed in the early pre-dawn.

Disclosure

When my mom checked in the morning and found me in my bed, I started crying and grabbed the note from behind my dresser to show her. In a blubbery snotty teary mess, I told her what happened.

What do you do about a child who was already grounded to his room for torturing his twin? It was obvious my mom was at a loss of what to do.

She told me how twice she'd had abortions prior to being pregnant with my twin and I: the first time she would have been showing at her wedding, and the second time she would have been unable to go on their honeymoon. We were the first "legitimate" pregnancy after our parents marriage.

My mom told me she'd always wanted two girls; that my brother was an accident. She'd even picked out a second girl's name (Samantha) but hadn't picked out any boy names.

She told me how my twin would howl for his babyish needs to be met, and that she always took care of him first because as long as

165

he'd stop crying, I'd stop crying. But heaven forbid she took care of me first, for he'd howl until his turn and carry on with his fit after. If he wanted a toy that was mine, he got it. If we were given two toys, he chose first. My mom told me that even at a few months old, I knew the other way around wasn't worth the tantrum. So she'd change/feed/whatever him first and send him to play with our older sister, and then she'd take care of me.

Sibling-Less

My mom decided from then on that I'd be raised a sibling-less child – a decision that changed the course of my life.

My sister and brother were often mistaken for "the twins" because they were so close. She told me to let them have each other.

The only time I would spend with my siblings was sitting in the bleachers next to my mom while she and I watched my sister's wrestling matches. (Of course my brother wasn't invited.)

She knew she was going to be around less and less as she worked to save money to get custody of us in the upcoming divorce. She did whatever was necessary to make sure I was safe. She taught me there would always be cash in her wallet when I needed it for my activities, and made me practice forging her name and her initials.

"How many nights and weekends can you fill with clubs and programs that would keep you safe, busy, and out of the house?" she asked me. And she drove me wherever I needed to go... even if that meant getting dropped off early or waiting hours for a ride home.

My teachers got behind my mom's mission to provide a safe space for me with all sorts of activities. They found ways to keep us safely separate during lunch and free periods, after school, evenings, and weekends.

Morning Bird

That was the first of many overnights at my neighbors. I also started waiting in their garage for the bus before school, waiting for the driver to be in sight before running to the pickup spot.

I became really good at being ready for school within minutes of opening my eyes. The quicker I could get dressed, grab my stuff and get out, the better. I learned to pack my backpack at night. I learned to wear my hair in a perpetual bun to hide my bedhead. I never mastered packing enough food for breakfast and lunch, so my mom started putting money on my school account for cafeteria lunches. She kept me supplied with boxes of granola bars to stash in my locker, and always had snacks waiting in her car.

Nightmares

But she couldn't protect me from my dreams. After fleeing my home in fear from my twin, I started having nightmares almost every night.

It was unsettling when my gentle peaceful goddess dreams shifted into nightmares where I was constantly running from attack. In my dreams, the pursuer wore the face of my brother or no face at all. Always running and hiding, knowing my life was in danger, the edge of hysteria bubbling below the surface, quieting my panicked breathing to not be discovered, throwing myself off moving trucks, escaping chains and locks, running endless corridors and never-ending hallways. Fear, so much fear. Always seconds away from my pursuer, from being killed.

My lucid dreamer brain could often recognize I was dreaming by the colors of the scene in front of me.... Cold shades of greys and muted earth tones. Sometimes there was a weird haze tinting outdoor scenes, like the sun was at war with a thick dust cloud, obscuring the shapes in front of me.

It was always my hands that alerted me to being stuck in a dream, trying to pick a lock, holding onto a door frame while seeing if the coast was clear, white knuckles gripping the kidnapper's car's bumper as I prayed for an unwatched moment to run. It was always seeing my hands that told me what I was experiencing wasn't real. And even though I couldn't understand how to end the dream, I knew I wasn't in real danger.

But knowing it wasn't real didn't stop the dreams. I couldn't wake myself up. Instead I had to keep playing the part, keep doing what I could to get safe inside the dream. Even though I was aware, the danger didn't stop. The threat would get worse if I focused on waking up instead of staying present to the imminent attacker at my heels.

It was still worse when I managed to wake myself up only to have the dream follow me into reality. Walking to the bathroom with shadows of my nightmares painted on the walls and darkness that nipped at my heels. When I really got stuck in the darkness of a nightmare, I'd turn on my light and stay awake as long as I could. Yet every blink of my eyes revealed the villains waiting patiently for me to return.

For the rest of my childhood, I didn't get a solid night's sleep. Every night I'd feel mortal danger lurking in my dreams. Do you know what it's like to wake up more tired than when you went to sleep? What it feels like to have every muscle shaking from running a marathon in your mind all night? To barely be able to walk because your muscles are so tired from sleep?

Design

Girl Scouts already kept me busy and out of the house, and had been a core aspect of my life for years. I especially loved how much time I'd get to spend with my mom. My mom was my Girl Scout leader, and we were a happy, active troop. In 6th grade, we focused on program development - working on designing and facilitating weekend events where hundreds of girls would cycle through different activities and earn a badge in one day or one weekend.

My first graphic design was published in the shape of patches for The Milwaukee Girl Scout Counsel. I remember feeling humbled and unworthy when I saw a box of thousands of patches, all with my design on them. I remember feeling thunderstruck when I was asked to design more.

I never saw my mom happier than when she was immersed in nature, teaching girls to be powerful strong women leaders. She taught us to sing to the fairies, how to trailblaze paths, and listen to the silence. We would walk when the moon was full, stargaze when the moon slept, and she showed us how to know the phases of the moon based on which of the three guides was present: the windy woman, the resting rabbit, and the laughing man.

It's too bad my siblings never got to meet that mom - the mom who smiled and laughed and hugged trees, the mom who exemplified embodied ownership.

Premonition Photographs

With such active dreams, I was so tired all the time from the nightmares and I started confusing awake and asleep. To sort out reality, I started keeping file folders of photographs in my mind to help me recognize a dream when it came to life.

Déjà vu became a regular aspect of daily life. These rerun dreams taught me to anticipate the before and after better. I could close my eyes - awake or asleep - and see what was to come.

Often these were mundane situations, just ordinary glimpses into everyday life. It always freaked people out when I would respond to what they were only thinking about saying.

I learned to trust what I didn't see. I'd spend hours studying the dream photos I knew I'd see again someday soon. But I didn't just look at the snapshot, I'd memorize the micro expressions each person wore in the picture so I could see what was happening outside of the frame.

More than once, these premonition dreams kept me safely out of the same hallways as my brother, avoiding insults and cruel words.

Performance

A friend encouraged me to join a literature interpretation competition program called *Forensics*. Until I started performing, I didn't understand that not everyone could hear the nuance and meaning of written text inside their head. When I read, I could hear the characters' voices, I could feel their emotions... or at least in the well written stuff, not the drivel school provided.

It was weeks into the season when I first joined, and everyone else had their performance pieces already chosen. There were many different types of categories that I could perform in, so my teacher chose some example readings in prose, poetry, humorous and dramatic interpretation categories.

I don't think I'll ever forget the look on my teacher's face when she watched me do cold-reads that first day on the Forensics team. There were stacks of prepared pieces, and my teacher chose things at random for me to read. A 30-second scan and then I'd read until she cut me off. After 3 performances, she went to a different stack and pulled out Old English poetry. As she handed me the poem, she told me to just guess at the pronunciations if I didn't know a word. The poem spoke to me - I could feel the writer's heart in his words and imagined him reading it to his love through my lips. It was the funniest thing watching my teacher's jaw drop lower with every line I spoke.

I didn't realize studying micro expressions in my dreams would help me read expression – both in text and in person. I learned I could adjust my performance based on how it was landing with the competition judges, even though they weren't supposed to let emotion show during the performance. Every time, without fail, I'd take home first place in my category – in every *Forensics* category I tried.

I was also encouraged to join choir and I earned a few gold medals in singing competitions too. I taught myself songs by quietly picking out tunes on my dad's piano. The whisper of my voice was barely loud enough to carry the melody to my ears.

I found it easy to sing in front of judges and perform in front of hundreds of people, earning dozens of shiny gold medals and blue ribbons. Yet I was terrified of being seen and heard at home.

Purposeful

No matter how hard I worked, one of my teachers never saw my writing fit to give me a grade above a B, no matter how many hours I spent researching, writing and rewriting. After yet another paper I'd spent a ridiculous amount of time writing still didn't earn an A, I was ready to give up. Instead, when we were assigned our next paper, I decided to find a way to fulfill his assignment while breaking all the set rules. We were assigned to write about someone in history we'd want to meet, what we'd ask them and why. We were given examples of football players, presidents, and movie stars. I was disgusted by the shallowness of the assignment. I decided to write the exact opposite of what he was asking for – I wrote a paper about how I wanted to meet Hitler to understand how he could kill 6 million Jews. It was the biggest slap in the face I could think of for this jerk of a teacher. It was the first A-grade my writing earned.

After that, I started writing for myself and not caring what the assignments were. From then on, I started caring more about how much I could learn despite the limitations of the education system. And what could be learned outside of formal education.

Sacred Wisdom

The dreams I looked forward to the most were when I was myself, and I'd be visited by another being, deity, or entity. I loved when I'd be visited by tree spirits, sprites, or fairies from wherever I'd meditated earlier in the day.

My science teacher swooned when I described a visit with Frost when he brought my first crystalline white window-scape for the winter, the fussy fuzzy detailed line art was exquisitely geometric.

And I especially loved when I'd get to meet Wisdom Keepers – people who were spiritual leaders, healers, Earth Mothers, Gods and Goddesses from many beliefs all around the world. I learned so much from those dreams.

Sometimes I could grasp enough of what I'd heard while traveling the world in my sleep that later I could look up words in other languages to figure out where I'd been. Because of these foreign dreams, I have recognized meaning of words in at least three languages that I don't speak.

My favorite dream was when North Wind would come visit me, and I'd ride on her robes as she cleared the sky for a crisp bright pink sunrise, tendrils of her honey colored hair in golden ribbons riding the air currents all around me. She showed me sacred geometry in nature, taught me how to lucid dream, and helped me understand the interconnectedness of all things.

Dream Stories

When my teacher read some of the dreams I'd written about in the margins of my notebook, I got called into her office. To my surprise, I wasn't in trouble. Instead, she invited me to be one of the editors of the school's poetry book (an invitation was usually reserved for 7th and 8th graders), and she had me take a permission slip to my mom.

My school published a poetry book each year, curated by a group of students. During the selection process, I was handed an envelope of poems and asked to pick which ones to publish and which to cut. With all the poems chosen, it was then time to start layout and I spent hours typing, checking grammar, spelling, and verifying what was going to print perfectly matched what the author had submitted.

Later that year, long after the school poetry book was finished, I was called into another private meeting with my teacher and my mom. My teacher handed me a big fat hardcover book with a royal blue cover and gold embossing. It was opened up to my dream poem. She had submitted my writing for a national poetry publication, and out of the hundreds of thousands of submissions I'd been chosen! I'll never forget what it felt like to have someone believe in me enough to share my words with the world.

Thank You, Trauma

It was a whirlwind twelve-months going from Special Education evaluation to becoming a nationally published author, award-winning performer, and book editor at the age of 12... all because of facing death and surviving.

How drastically altered life can be after any type of trauma. The beauty is in honoring the gratitude for all that trauma gives us.

Those middle school hobbies were the start of a passionate purpose-driven career that has me excited to start every day. In hindsight, that year was the start of everything that I do today. And I couldn't be more grateful for this path in life.

Separation

A few years ago, I tried to speak to my twin about *The Chase* and how profoundly it altered the course of my life.

"Why do you always bring that up? It was one time. Just stop."

A few months later, he nonchalantly pointed a loaded gun at my chest, finger on the trigger.

It took over a year to disentangle our lives. At the time, I was running my brother's online business and it was my sole income. A decade earlier, I'd bought his pen name as a URL and built him a website for a Christmas gift. He had someone else running an ecommerce website on a different URL, but they fired my brother as a client at the start of Covid, shutting down the site with no transfer option. So I re-built his online store, re-photographed all of his products, and restructured his virtual sales system. Then I continued to manage the tech side of the company, running the newsletter, making graphics for marketing, and doing all sorts of other online business manager type tasks.

The Beginning

About a month after looking into the barrel of a gun, I found myself facing the possibility of death again. The doctor found a freckle in my eye that was either just a freckle or, based on my family medical history, meant I had about 6 months left to live. And it would take weeks to figure out my fate.

I was so grateful Michelle Bee happened to be offering a process called Healing Words, during the weeks I waited for diagnosis. What surprised me most along her journaling journey was when I went to write down a phrase that Michelle said: *I am <u>comforted</u> by my own power to heal.* But what I wrote was: *I am <u>confronted</u> by my own power to heal.*

It stopped me cold. Frozen in place, I stood transfixed. Both statements true, I couldn't erase either. They echoed in my mind, over and over, like a mantra stuck on repeat. Then the clarity came: if I had six months to live then I wanted to spend it helping my clients write and publish their books, and I would write my memoir alongside them.

It inspired me to create what I call *Hybrid Publishing*, where the imprint "Ritz Books" publishes your book, yet it's managed from your own Amazon account so you get 100% of the royalties and complete control post-publishing. That way, who cares how long I live... you'd always have control of your book printing and profits.

Ritz Books isn't just publishing, it's also ghostwriting and editing during the writing process, as well as cover design and interior layout. Many of my authors call me their *Book Doula*, birthing ideas into the world that they've been pregnant with for years or even decades. I have loved learning how to code both manuscripts and covers for seamless Search Engine Optimization (SEO) integration between Amazon, Google, your website, and social media, how it boosts the chances of becoming an instant bestselling author.

And when I shared my idea with my mailing list, the first to say yes was the writer who chose "Ritz Books" as my imprint five years before for her second book. The second yes was from the only other Ritz Books author, who also signed on to write her second book. Michelle's *Healing Words* book was the third yes. And within hours, the first group of Hybrid Publishing Ritz Books authors was full. It's been a whirlwind journey publishing 22 books over the first three years, with at least six more set to release in 2024. I couldn't be more grateful for what led me to where I am today.

Auntie's Prophesy

It was a year before I told anyone (besides my sister) about looking down the barrel of that gun. I didn't tell a soul until I dreamed *Auntie's Prophesy*... I dreamt that not only for myself, but for the benefit of his child, we could no longer be a part of each other's lives. I dreamed that if I stayed in his life, something would split him from his partner and the child would be raised fatherless. There's no doubt I bring out the worst in him, and the next generation deserves the best from her dad. So I took the knife from his hand and I cut the ties binding us together, separating our lives completely so he could cleanly walk forward with his daughter.

What I didn't expect was for my friends (and therapist) to adamantly agree with a prophesy dream I'd just had – each and every person insisting I remove him from my life completely and forever, offering whatever support was needed to sever ties. I still grieve for the loss of my living twin. And I will forever be grateful for the gifts trauma gave me. I feel lucky to have found my life path at such a young age; I've found it richly rewarding to help so many people share their stories. How grateful I am to be alive and telling you this true tale.

Turn your stories into leads, a legacy, and a business platform

If you're like most aspiring authors, there's a book inside of you waiting to be written that will transform the lives of your readers. The best part? Your book can help you build a profitable business. I created Hybrid Publishing for transformational authors and artists who are serious about getting their message out to the world, who want to grow their business in sustainable and mindful ways, and who are seeking a spiritually rich and personally rewarding experience. Please don't wait until you're staring down the barrel of a gun or facing a cancer diagnosis - tomorrow isn't guaranteed! Start the journey today! www.StephRitz.com

What would it look like if you were to write a love letter to your trauma, thanking it for the gifts it gave you?

The Wounded Embryo
Hasti Fashandi, ND

Immigrating to the great United States of America as a refugee fleeing from a war-torn country was no easy feat. Were it not for my incredibly brave uncle, my family would never have been able to escape. Being an Iranian-American has been a beautiful thing, because not only did I grow up with such an incredibly rich culture all around me with parents who were very proud to be Iranian and made sure we knew how to speak our language, but I also got to experience the best parts of American life.

There were many traumatic barriers and experiences that each of the members of my family had to overcome in order to make it out; however, each and every one of us has an entirely unique lived experience of the same sets of traumatic events. It is in these ways in which we are similar, and yet so very much individual and distinct, where the beauty lies among us. For the majority of my years, I have had very skewed and misaligned views of myself and of those around me; however, throughout the journey of my experiences, I have come to learn that humans are beautiful and imperfect beings who essentially know not what they do. We are all just truly doing the very best we can, given our own unique sets of experiences and overall perspective of our world view. This way of thinking has helped to free me from mental chains that have been passed down through generations upon generations.

In elementary school, I remember Steph putting her face against my neighbor's horse's face and just breathing with him. It was one of the most beautiful connections that I had ever experienced between a human and animal at that point in my young age, but I still remember what Steph said, which was how this type of breathing with the horse helped them to connect with you, and imprint with you as a human that they have a connection with.

~ Hasti

Dr. Hasti Fashandi is an Iranian-American Naturopathic Doctor who was born in Tehran in 1984 during the eight-year war between Iran and Iraq. She is the youngest of three daughters and moved to the U.S. early in 1987, where she lived in Toledo before relocating to Milwaukee.

She grew up in Glendale with parents who spoke only Farsi in the home in an effort to preserve their native language. She attended undergrad in the Midwest before relocating to the West Coast, and ended up in Seattle for Naturopathic Medical school. After completing her residency, she gave birth to a beautiful baby girl, and is now living in the CA Bay Area as a single mother and business owner. When her daughter was 5, she made the bold decision to break generational chains and file for divorce. This decision led to the most difficult time of her life, but also the most rewarding.

https://drhastifashandi.com/

I am sitting here inside Peet's Coffee Shop on a beautiful, bright, sunny Saturday morning; I close my eyes and check-in for a moment. I can feel my heart racing, and my hands feel a bit clammy; I am noticing the anxiety that has been fluttering in the pit of my very soul for what feels like an eternity. Today it's about my work and whether or not I'm charging what I'm worth, considering every other provider I know has raised their rates annually, and I've kept mine the same since 2018 and am struggling to make ends meet; yesterday it was about whether or not my daughter's father might try to kidnap her and take her internationally after the threats he left me with when I was leaving him, and who knows what will take over me tomorrow?

As I think back to my very conception, I would be foolish not to take stock of the massive levels of stress hormones that my own mother had coursing through her veins at that very moment. I was born in 1984 in Tehran, Iran during the war between Iran and Iraq that lasted from 1980 – 1988. What I do know is that I personally have no memories of my own from that period of time; however, as I have grown and moved through these 39 years on Earth, I have come to understand a lot of what has been holding me back in my life, ever since before I was even born.

To begin, one would imagine that we would begin at the beginning, but what is considered the 'beginning'? Where does one even begin such a story? I suppose the easiest place to start would be to say that I am the youngest of three girls. My oldest sister was born in 1981, my middle sister was born in 1982, and I was born in 1984. We were all conceived very close to one another, and let's just say that the second and third children were not planned. Considering the fact that my parents were living in Iran during a time when not only was Saddam Hussein dropping carpet bombs all across the capital city of Tehran, housing millions of innocent civilians, but they were also just coming out of a horrific revolution with the overthrowing of Mohammad Reza Shah, and the Islamic stronghold that Ayatollah Ruhollah Khomeini's rule was bringing to Iran.

When you have nothing but daughters in an Islamically-ruled patriarchal country, you immediately realize that they have no hope of a future in a land where women are oppressed and viewed as mere possessions to be owned. Although Iran was once a free nation under the Shah's dynasty, with men and women being viewed as equals, and women having the freedom to dress however they pleased, once the Shah was kicked out of Iran and the religious Islamic leaders took his place, things shifted very quickly. Women were no longer allowed to leave their homes without covering their hair. If they wore pants that were too tightly fitting, they had to make sure that they wore a long coat or robe to cover all of the parts of fabric that were clinging. If they had any makeup on, or were attractive in any way to entice a male's attention, the women were the ones seen as the wrongdoers. Eventually, Khomeini developed a very deadly army of militants who would line the streets bearing AK-47 rifles just to scare civilians into following their strong-armed rule. If you were a woman seen walking in the street with your head scarf sitting too far back on your head, you could be arrested and charged. Even if you were a female seen in public with a male, if you were pulled over or questioned by the Islamic Republic's military, you had to show proof of your marriage license, or somehow otherwise prove that you were a blood relative of the person you were with; dating was literally banned by law. Males and females were no longer allowed to be friends and mingle with one another in public without the fear of reprimand based off of "what relation the two had to one another".

Given the state of the country as a whole during this period of time, after my parents had their first daughter, they were already starting to devise a plan for an escape route for themselves and their child. However, shortly after they had their first, they had a second daughter, which became even more of a reason to get everyone out, and unfortunately, before they had the chance to evacuate the country, my mother got pregnant yet again... This time, with me.

By this time, my parents were navigating air raid sirens going off at a moment's notice, which would leave the darkest and most eerily silent city of millions of people that you could ever imagine. It was as though someone had dropped a massively thick monstrosity of a blanket over all of the innocent men, women, and children living in Tehran, almost as if to cover and protect them from the fighter jets and bombers.

The stories I have heard are of my mother fumbling with

flashlights underneath her clothing, just to have enough light to feed her hungry children, or my father getting stuck in a blinding darkness, while driving his family across town, to the point where he had one foot outside of the driver's door, just to make sure he wasn't moving too fast and didn't accidentally hit a pedestrian. It was these horrific living conditions that fueled my parents' intense desire to escape and attempt to evacuate their family from the increasingly dark grip that had taken over their homeland.

When my mother learned that she was pregnant for a third time, my parents were already planning their exit from Tehran, and the thought of evacuating a family of five, compared to a family of four, started to weigh more heavily on them. Given the type of crisis situation that was constantly happening within my mother's psyche from even before conception, not only did every single one of her unfertilized eggs feel, experience, witness, and absorb every terrifying event, but the constant stress that both of my parents were under when they conceived me had been exponentially mounting from the day my oldest sister came into this world. Is it any wonder, then, how a developing fetus within her mother's womb can be deeply impacted by all that is occurring in the world around her, right outside of her mother's belly? It's not a question of whether or not my conscious mind and memory are able to recall any of this, as this is an easy answer; of course, I have no conscious memories of being in the womb. That being said, if we think about human development beginning within the mother's womb, every single event that a human being experiences from conception, and possibly even before, from what is passed down energetically into the egg that becomes fertilized, until they die, will inevitably shape their perceptions of the world around them.

The ways that we know this to be true are from habitual patterns that set off similar alarm signals within our nervous system, which may mimic a memory of being bombed, even if I was in my mother's belly when this event was happening. I have also been told that when I was around 3 years of age, which would have been when we were living in an apartment in Toledo, Ohio when thunderstorms used to hit, I would experience PTSD from the memory of bombs dropping all around us. I do actually have a distinct memory of my own of being very afraid of living in that Toledo apartment complex because of all of the noises and sounds that constantly surrounded us, which triggered my fears and anxieties. Now, when I think about my own 7-year-old daughter who is basically a carbon-copy of her Mama, she also has deeply-seated and inexplicable irrational fears of sounds that she hears from neighbors coming and going, kids playing in the courtyard, dogs jumping around or running in the apartment unit above us. This, in some ways, helps me to understand that she was in fact present during, and bore witness to, those exact fears and experiences that I went through when I was very young. A woman is in fact born with all of the eggs that she will ever have the ability to fertilize throughout her child-bearing years. Every single experience that she has throughout her lifetime, up until fertilizing that egg, will in some way, shape, or form, energetically enter that eventual fertilized being of a soul. My daughter actually has a lot of the same fears as I did growing up, and she has never had any knowledge that her mother carried, and in fact at times, still does carry, many of those exact same fears.

Speaking of fear, we could get very deep into this emotion; however, the aspect of fear that seems the most relevant here are the fears that are passed down to us from our parents and ancestors, which can accumulate over the course of our lives. This is especially true if we are not mindful of which emotions we experience as being our own, and consciously separate them out from all of the other "stuff" that is of the universe, collective human consciousness, and the ether that does not belong to us. So much of the weight that we carry in our day-to-day lives truly does not belong to us; it is a karmic imprint of a life cycle that has been passed down to us from generations of our ancestors who walked this Earth before us. There is still, of course, all of what occurs in our present day in every corner of the world, which impacts each and every one of us, as well. Whether we are aware of it or not, the blood that is spilled in Ukraine, Palestine, Iran, and countless other nations across this globe, absolutely impacts our collective human consciousness in ways that can be difficult to shake if we are not careful about what we allow into our energetic spheres, and how we are able separate those feelings and emotions out from our own.

Fear is the emotion that seems to have ruled me the most strongly since prior to my induction into this world. Not only was I born in a war-zone, but because the Iranian government would not allow families to flee the country out of the fear that they would not return, my family had to break apart just to be able to escape our war-torn homeland. My parents had to fake a divorce, and of course, in a patriarchal country ruled by men, a mother has no right to her children; therefore, my father was the one allowed permission to take his three daughters out of the country, while my mother was left behind to fend on her own.

Imagine being a mother to three young children, all under the age of 5 years, and suddenly being ripped from them because you are not allowed to travel out of the country with them. It was in fact my uncle, my father's brother, who has sadly since passed, and who had excelled in his premedical studies and graduate coursework, who had been sponsored to come to the US to study medicine. He was living in Wisconsin at the time, and it was him who ended up sponsoring us and supporting our escape with refugee status out of Tehran. That being said, none of us had any papers that allowed us to enter the US, aside from what my uncle had prepared for us; however, my helpless mother had nothing and nobody to fall back on, or to help her get out. My uncle did indeed plan on sponsoring her, as well; however, due to the difficulties with translation and her lack of paperwork, my mother ended up getting stuck in France for almost a year. By the time she made it to Toledo, Ohio, which was where my father's eldest brother was living at the time, and was reunited with her three children, so much time had passed that I did not even remember who she was anymore. Again, I have no personal memory of this; however, I was told that when I saw my mother, being the youngest and having forgotten who she was, instead of embracing her after all that time, I was in fact afraid of her, and I was crying while hiding behind my paternal grandmother.

Now that I am a mother of a 7-year-old daughter, I cannot even fathom the heartbreak this must have caused my mother back then. It never even occurred to me, until I became a mother, just how difficult that period of time must have been for my own mom. The separation from her children, the inability to speak European languages, as she was forced to travel to make her way through Amsterdam and France, and eventually to the US, just to be reunited with her three young babies.

Over the months, our family became a more "normal" unit again, with the five of us living in one apartment unit, and my father's eldest brother, his wife, and my paternal grandmother living in the unit across the hallway. I don't remember much from that period of time; with the exception of fears of the dark, people's voices outside of our balcony door, car alarms going off in the middle of the night, and I also have a very random, yet vivid memory that each individual section of the apartment building was color-coded by different bright colors, decked out with 80s shag carpets to match.

We lived in Toledo for about three years, where we learned about and celebrated Christmas for the first time with my uncle's family before we transitioned to Milwaukee, WI in 1990 to live with my other uncle, my father's middle brother. It was right around the time when we had just moved to Milwaukee when Jeffrey Dahmer (A.K.A. The Milwaukee Cannibal) was in the news. Can you imagine the fear and terror my parents must have been experiencing at that time, having just recently moved to the States; now they were living in a city with a serial killer that they had to protect their children against.

If you knew my sisters and me back in the day, you also most certainly knew that my parents, namely my father, were incredibly strict. Not only were we never allowed to have sleepovers at our friend's houses, but even as we got older, we were not allowed to leave the house if it was already starting to get dark outside. In hindsight, it is evident that the fears that were fueling the behaviors of my parents toward us during our primitive years, were clearly meant to both keep us safe, as well as to "keep us on track".

The pressures that were placed on my sisters and me were one of needing to become educated and to succeed. Our studies and career tracks were of the utmost importance, to the point where not much else mattered. When boys called our house in high school, they were grilled with countless questions about who they were, what relation they had to us, and what their intentions were for calling us. Needless to say, none of us were ever allowed to date until we left home for college.

When you think about having abandoned your homeland to come

to a foreign country so that your daughters could live safely, and where they'd have all of the same opportunities for freedom, learning, and growing as their male counterparts, there is a great deal of responsibility that comes along with this. The expectations that parents can place on their children in this regard can inadvertently leave the child with a sense of uneasiness and urgency, which is oftentimes translated from the parent to the child. My sisters and I would all agree that there was quite a bit of pressure put on us by our parents to make sure that we took advantage of all of the opportunities presented to us that this great land had to offer; however, what we ended up experiencing was a significant amount of anxiety from these pressures.

We had some pretty big shoes to fill, with doctors and surgeons on both sides of our family, most Persian parents pushed their children to study in the fields of medicine, law, or engineering. My father always pushed schooling and education; he always said, as long as your mind is rich, your life will also be rich. My family pushed us to higher degrees of education because they did not have the same opportunities afforded to them in Iran. The education system is very different back home; you do not choose your major, but are placed into a predetermined major based upon how you place in the national college placement exam. When kids are 17-18 years of age, during their last year of high school, they take a week-long exam that tests their knowledge in almost every single field of study. Then, based on how well they place in the different sections of this national exam, the educational board then decides on what their major field of study will be in college. For example, my middle uncle was placed in the medical field, while my father was placed in agricultural engineering. Interestingly, they each did astoundingly well in their respective areas of study; however, it can seem like such a shift in our thinking to perceive the idea of someone other than ourselves dictating our career future paths.

I sometimes think about the series of events that have taken place over the course of my life, all of which have brought me to this exact moment; the person I am in this world, and the type of mother, sister, daughter, niece, doctor, and friend that I am is essentially a product of all of the experiences that have brought me to this point. So many of the fears that I grew up with as a child were not fears of my own, but those of my parents and other adults around me, which were passed onto me. For example, some of the seeds of my lifelong fear of failure were planted by my parents' expectations of my grades in school.

I believe that many of us have very similar fears of failing, or not living up to our full potential in life; however, how much of these fears are truly our own? How many fears do we have walking through life that have trickled into our psyches from the ways in which we were raised? Not only that, but how can some of these difficult and harsh energies influence the collective human consciousness as a whole? I occasionally think back to the type of relationship that I had with my siblings growing up, and I have many memories of harsh and negative things being said to one another; however, we were so unaware of how we were carrying those negative energies forth with others we came across, as well. Therefore, a harsh word from one of my sisters may have been enough to put me into a mood where I would perhaps take it out on my friend, and that then trickles into the subconscious of our world. How we treat one another, and truly, how we treat ourselves, in many ways is shaped and determined by the ways in which our loved ones and the people closest to us speak to us and treat us. The ways in which we grow up, and how we allow others to interact with us, actually creates and sets up an energy of what we allow into our psyches from a very young age.

Interestingly, even though siblings are generally all raised under the same roof, they can come out of their childhoods and enter the world with very different and skewed ideas and memories of their upbringing together. Oftentimes, there are aspects of the nuclear family unit that are very unique and individual, depending upon which child is asked the questions. In other words, one sibling might have received much more backlash from a parent than the other siblings for instance, or perhaps either the father or mother were much more willing to allow only one of their children to bear witness to the difficulties and issues of the marriage or issues with in-laws.

People may look at siblings and think, "How could you have ever been raised in the same household?" but what we don't realize is that each sibling likely endured their own unique sets of traumas that may not have actually been shared among the siblings as a whole. I know of families where only the youngest son bore witness to key atrocities, such as their mother being physically attacked and harmed by their father; however, although all of the siblings in the home may have felt like they witnessed the same incident, only the child who physically saw with his own eyes has truly witnessed the event.

Much of this understanding has helped me to learn and grow from some of the negative memories that I have from my own childhood. As an adult, and now mother myself, I understand how each individual's unique experiences throughout their lives can impact the lives of those around them, either in a positive or negative manner. Although we may have no idea how our interactions with others carry them through the world and what downstream impacts it can have on others in the world, we need to be mindful of the fact that everyone is dealing with the weight of their own worlds. In this way, it is important to keep in mind that we are all doing the very best that we can at any given moment in time.

I deeply believe that we are all intrinsically good people within our heart of hearts; I feel that there are experiences that we have throughout the course of our lives that shape the way we interact with others, as well as how much we let people into our lives and our beings. I also believe that nobody wakes up wanting to face the world in a negative or ill manner. I truly believe that we do the best that we can with the resources that are afforded to us. However, what we do or don't have is more subjective than it is objective. In other words, what one person considers "rich" and "happy" will most certainly not be the next person's idea or definition of these words, by a long shot.

It is for this reason that we must always remember that all people come from different walks of life; even those who appear to be related and were raised in the same household and with the same nuclear family typically end up being very unique and oftentimes very different individuals. I have struggled in life with many thoughts about myself that I deeply believed or felt about my own sense of self-worth. However, when I really sit and dissect where these sets of core beliefs originated from, I realize that much of it stems from the fears of my family members that were absorbed by me, as well as the ways in which others interacted with me and what I allowed them to say to me. When I say "allowed," I mostly mean "accepted to be true".

At this point, it seems like a good a time as ever to shift our focus to how much of these energies are in fact passed down to us, or perhaps through us, from our elders and ancestors. There are certain cultures and regions of the world where happiness is in fact shunned or even considered a crime, and things like sulking and sobbing and depression are common practice and in fact encouraged. As insane as this may sound, back home in Iran, there are more "celebrations" for dead Islamic religious prophets than there are "celebrations or parties" around birthdays or people's lives.

Young adolescents and adults have been imprisoned and flagellated for dancing and singing in the park or streets, or even just playing happy music in public in Tehran. Meanwhile, public shows of self-flagellation and mourning during the celebration of the death of the prophet Muhammad's grandson, are in fact encouraged by the Iranian government.

This type of suppression of happy displays of human emotion, and support of only the emotions of grief and fear and sadness, over countless generations inevitably impacts the collective human consciousness and psyche of each subsequent generation. It is inevitable that this sad, grieving, depressed energy will pass through to our offspring, in the same way that the human genetic code passes information from parent to child.

Growing up, I used to think this type of detrimental and catastrophic thinking was normal. For example, hearing my parents or grandparents discuss every seeming topic in their lives in terms of "woe is me" became an exhausting part of our daily lives. It never occurred to me when I was growing up, just how much of this learned behavior I was internalizing; however, as I watched my grandmothers speak this way, and both my mother and father speak this way, I started to realize that this is a form of generational trauma that gets passed down by the elders we grow up around. Much of this learned behavior can also be perpetuated among the siblings in a household, as well.

I used to think that no matter how old I got, the members of my family would never be able to see any other version of me than "the little baby of the family who can't do a single thing for herself". When it finally occurred to me that I had been perpetuating the same generational cycles and trauma that had been passed to me in the ways that my marriage was so negatively impacting my child, I had to do something about it. However, when it came to my family members, there was not always unconditional support. I do not blame them for this, for again, there have been so many cultural taboos and judgments that have been passed down from generation to generation, that I can understand why they had their line of thinking. That being said; however, there came a moment during motherhood for me, which was when my daughter was about 4-5 years of age, where I realized that if I did not get out, and quickly, there would be no way that I could protect my child from repeating the same mistakes I watched my mother make.

When I decided that I was going to leave my marriage and relationship of 16 years, just 3 short months after having purchased a family home with a 5-year-old daughter, I knew I had to move quickly while I had the will in me to get it done. I had many fears about what my ex-husband may or may not have done at that particular moment; however, I had to swiftly move out of our home and start a shared custody schedule for my daughter with her father. I filed for divorce shortly after this, and although this period of my life was by far the absolute most difficult time for me in my 39-year life thus far, it was made even more difficult due to feeling very alone in my decision to leave. Unfortunately, when you have been raised in a culture where other people's opinions matter more than your own, it is understandable why parents or siblings might not be 100% fully supportive of your decision. I mean, being a single mother in the Bay Area of California while trying to run a small business and private medical practice is not an easy feat, and yet, women who raise children on their own are somehow below or beneath a married woman with children in the Iranian culture. The only thing worse than souring as an independent single woman who never gets married in our culture is being a single divorced working mother; nobody will ever want you then!

I dealt with a lot of painful and difficult truths about my family members during that time; it was almost like a relearning of who these people were to me, as there were some major perspective shifts from my thought processes, as compared to my relationship with them while I was a kid growing up. I even came to find out later that some of my parents' closest friends were shocked or appalled at my decision, because "the Hasti they knew would have been able to make her marriage work for the sake of her child". What some of these very people do not understand is that it was for the sake of my child that I actually left her father, so that she would not follow in my footsteps and make the same mistakes as I did. I essentially married my father, thinking that that was the type of man that I needed in my life in order to feel safe, secure, and taken care of; however, what I never fully appreciated was that the same way that I had to be or act like someone different around my father, I ended up having to be an entirely different person from the Hasti inside around my ex-husband, as well.

I'd like to switch the focus to my sisters for a moment. I love and adore my sisters, as I know that they feel the same way about me, being that I am the youngest of the three. Although I know that everything they do and say is in the interest of what is best for me, sometimes it feels very unsupportive and detrimental to any attempt at progress being made in my life. At times, I feel like now that my parents are at such an old age, where their health and mobility are beginning to be compromised, the thoughts that used to preoccupy their minds about the choices and mistakes of their daughters have become increasingly trivial with every passing hospital visit. It never would have occurred to me that at some point in our adult lives, our siblings sort of take over their place and essentially become our parents, especially for the younger members of the family unit.

I have struggled throughout life with fully comprehending what it means for each of us to walk a very unique and individual path throughout our lives; however, when I think about the unconditional love that our mother provided to all three of us daughters, and yet, how differently each of us has grown throughout our older adulthood, it is astonishing to me. I understand that I am the youngest of three, and I understand that the people in my family believe that there are things that are still expected of me, but I also now understand so much more than I did just a short three years ago. Since my divorce, it has become clear to me that it was truly during my darkest hours, when I could see the true guttural fear in those who loved me the most. What I mean by this is that, although my closest family members may have said things to me that were hurtful in the moment, it was only their fear of what might happen to me, or where I might end up, that made them say those things. It was all of the fears, i.e. of judgment, of regret, of financial ruin, of loss of honor, of embarrassment, that created someone other than that I have ever known for my life, to speak to me with such disdain and lack of support.

I also now understand that the interactions that my parents carried out with me and my siblings were not one and the same. I know for a fact that my father had an entirely different relationship with my middle sister than he did with my oldest sister and myself. I also know that my mother has had a different type of relationship with me than she has had with my older sisters. When we were younger, we used to say "Mom and Dad don't love us equally," when really, it was not that they loved us any more or less than one another, but that their relationships and interactions with each of us were individual and unique. Ever since we were young and growing up, there have been things that my siblings have seen and known about our family unit, family life, and parental relationship that I may never know or hear throughout my entire life. I know that there is a lot to my family, and not just our nuclear family, but I also know that we are not unique in this fact, nor are we unique in the sense that oftentimes siblings grow up to know and appreciate an entirely differing and alternate version of their mothers and fathers than one another.

To be honest, this feels more normal to me than trying to pretend like none of us have any real trauma in our lives, or that we lead some semblance of a perfect life. Life is messy, and humans are by nature imperfect, otherwise "To err is to be human" would not exist. Perhaps if we could all just learn to be a little bit more honest with ourselves, as well as with those who we love around us, then we would all benefit so much more than if we continue to lead with fear.

Anyway, it's now about 2.5 years since the date that I packed my bags and moved out of that house that had the darkest cloud over it for me and left with the most minimal and basic supplies or furniture, into an 860-square-foot apartment in San Jose, CA. I am sitting at an amazing local restaurant called Aqui enjoying some chips and guacamole while I finish this chapter in this beautifully incredible book that I am so very honored to be a part of. My daughter and I are now living in a 2-bedroom, 2-bathroom two-story condo that we just adore in Mountain View, CA and I have been in private practice and fully working for myself in my own business now for over a year! I can easily say that I am so proud of myself! When I think back, I honestly don't even know how I made it, but by the infinite universe and better powers at be, and most importantly, my incredibly beastly strong ancestors, I have made it. And I am not only making it, I am thriving! My daughter and I have started a YouTube channel together, I am a locally well-known naturopathic and functional medicine doctor, and thanks in large part to my ex-husband, I own my own business and have been blessed to be able to work for myself.

My practice has recently been expanding, and things finally feel really good and more than okay than I have in a very long time. I have to say though, that it was not until I went on my week-long spiritual retreat to the Sacred Valley in Peru that I truly awoke to the full understanding of what our beings truly go through in this life. I spent a week fully immersed in Peruvian plant medicine and came out of that experience an entirely different person. What drove me to Peru in the first place was the feeling that even though I had removed myself from the life that I felt had been suffocating me for almost two entire decades, I was still not the mother that I knew I had the capability of being to my beautiful and brilliant daughter.

Emma Madison Bou-Reslan, the entire reason that mommy's EMBR Naturopathic Medicine & Apothecary business even exists, everything I do in my life is for you, and only you.

I know that sounds so incredibly sacrificial, but it is not. Never before had I realized how important the happiness and health of Emma's mother and father are to her entire well-being. My beautiful 7-year-old daughter has tics. She has been diagnosed with Tourette's Disease, and I can recall back to when she was three years of age when they first started. This tiny only newly developed being in this world has already had to experience the pain of parents going through a divorce. She used to tell me when she was younger and when her father and I still lived together, "Mommy, it feels like there is a rope between you and Daddy". Well, even now, over two years later, where she alternates between her dad's and my house every 2-3 days, with alternating weekends, she still tells me, "Mommy, it still feels like there is a rope between you and Daddy".

Does it break my entire heart when I hear her say things like this to me? Absolutely! You better believe it does! But, do I also find comfort and solace in the fact that I know without a shadow of a doubt that her father and I brought the literal worst out in one another? Yes, he and I had gotten to a scary point, where we were completely not the right versions of ourselves in front of our daughter. No matter how hard we tried, we just could not control ourselves around her. During the COVID pandemic lockdown, so much got to an entirely peaked crescendo within our household, that I felt as though I had to walk around on eggshells just so that I didn't rock the boat too much.

The morning that I moved my small U-Haul worth of things out of our recently purchased home, I was literally terrified. You know, my ex-husband never understood the type of guttural fear he instilled within me. Did he ever truly do anything to warrant that level of a response from me? Absolutely not! Never was he physically abusive or harmful to me in any way. However, there was just something about the way he reacted to things in life, which I now realize were his own unhealed traumas and wounds. His high-alert and on-guard self that felt as though he needed to strongly protect himself. You know, we get these survival instincts from our ancestors.

So, it is not always a bad thing; however, I digress. After having been with him for almost 20 years, and after everything we had been through with our families and just all of the ups and downs, and truly having brought out the worst of the worst in one another, I felt scared for my well-being the day that I was moving my things out of that house. That was the day he finally knew. He finally realized on that day that I had had enough. I was done!

My therapist once told me, "In order to break the cycles of generational trauma, you need to realize and fully understand that your parents did things or said things to you that were indeed harmful and traumatic, and that it was not okay". It was in the "it was not okay" part where the emphasis was being made. She knew that I had always made excuses for my parents, because I have known and seen the difficulties and struggles of raising children in a foreign place with minimal family or support. It was my therapist's ability to see in me that I did not fully recognize the "it was not okay" part, as she proceeded to explain that it is only with this understanding where parents are able to stop the cycle of harm that we pass to our own children. These words went off like a bomb in my head and her words still reverberate throughout my ears. What she said to me made me fully aware and empathetic to the fact that I had been doing and saying things to my own daughter that were harmful and also not okay. I am grateful that she shared this perspective with me, as it has helped me to catch myself during similar moments with my daughter.

All I can say at this point in my life is that I am so incredibly grateful for having had the experiences that have shaped the person I have become. Yes, I am a mother, and yes, I needed to do better; however, never did it occur to me that doing better also meant a complete upheaval and reassessment of my entire life. Today I can say with the highest level of confidence that my daughter and I are finally on the other side. All I need to do moving forward through any struggle is to just remind myself of how far we have come. Time heals all wounds, and we have been blessed with a beautiful combination of healing and growing as a result of the trauma and pain.

Learning to Love Myself
Kimberly Omiseun Early

As a trainer, I work on merging the worlds of ECE, spirituality and Social – Emotional Learning (SEL) with both children and adults.

My strength lies in allowing people to see the Power of their words, especially recognizing the impact of what they say to young children.

I have been sought out as a trainer, since my trainings provide intentional, intensive, and reflective teaching around the lenses of equity and cultural responsiveness to understand the specific needs of children.

This chapter is about what I faced and experienced with the carelessness of a teacher in third grade. Words and their impact on people, particularly our youngest ones and how we can easy carry this trauma into adulthood. As a result of this, I have dedicated this aspect of my life to helping others not make that same mistake and instead work toward how to make the world a better place.

As the Founder and CEO of Pearls of Wisdom LLC, (which is named after my grandmother, Pearl Early) I dedicated my business to anti-bias, cultural relevancy and mindfulness.

www.pearlsofwisdomllc.org

Kimberly Early, also known as, Iya Ifabunkunmi Omiseun Ponmile Fayemi Akanbi omo Beulah, is a Priest of Ifa and Yemoja and was initiated in Abeokuta, Nigeria in 2020. She is a mother, community activist and Reiki Master with 29 years of teaching experience. Omiseun works in the Early Childhood Education (ECE) field and for 18 years, has taught in the education department at Highline College. She graduated from Pacific Oaks College NW with a Teaching Certificate and Masters in Human Development.

Omiseun's volunteer work includes centering social justice around Black children, working towards ending systematic racism by making changes to policies that improve the life of Black children. As a trainer, she works on merging the worlds of ECE, spirituality and Social – Emotional Learning (SEL). She likes to travel, dance and spend time with family and friends. Her proudest accomplishment is being the mother of her brilliant son, Quentin, IfaDahunce!

The instant I met Kimberly, I walked up to her like an old friend and starting chatting this vivacious giggle and soulful woman up, trying to figure out where we'd met before. Turns out we'd never met. But my soul knew her, recognized her, and I was drawn to learn more.

Steph Ritz

I was born in Brooklyn, New York and while attending elementary school, is where I learned to not like my beautiful dark skin. School during this age from age 6 to 11 should be a time of loving and exploring who you are – children should not be made to feel ashamed of who they are or dislike themselves, but during this time is when it started. I grew up in a row house of three story brownstones and come from a family with three older brothers – I am the youngest and the only girl. As I like to say, "their favorite sister!" (It doesn't matter that I am the only girl – that is besides the point). I come from a loving, affectionate and caring home and had a really good childhood!

Most times, my house was filled with laughter since my family loves to have a good time, joke and play. It always seemed like someone was home and lots of family members would come to visit us. Even though my mom and dad lived in separate houses, my father was very involved in my life, coming over to play Old Maid with me, take me the movies or picking me up to take me to dance class at F and G Dance Studio as we rode the #45 bus into downtown Brooklyn.

I would go to Pittsburgh every summer to see my family, since both of my parents were born and raised there and a couple of times, I recall taking the Greyhound bus to Atlantic City for vacation, when it was more of a family spot. We rode bikes down the boardwalk, played on the beach, went on carnival rides like roller coasters and the scrambler, when those rides were e located on part of the boardwalks which stretched out into the Jersey shore.

Growing up in Crown Heights, I have found memories of the huge oak tree in the middle of the block. If you ran past it during the summer with your mouth open, gnats would fly into your mouth! I loved to hear the beautiful summertime call of the ice cream truck, with soft serve ice cream coming to your block. Playing games outside like hopscotch and double Dutch – and though I could never really jump well, I was a really good turner! In my household, I am the darkest in skin color among my siblings, but no one in my family ever teased me or made me feel bad about my skin color, so I felt pretty secure at home with who I was. In addition, on both sides of my family, we range in color from a light almond color to a rich deep coffee – it's a beautiful range of hues!

Just before I started third grade, my mom switched my school from a public school to a private school in the community. She transferred me because there was a bully at the school, a little boy, who was picking on other children. He would go around, beating up other kids and I happened to be one of the targets. Since his mother worked at the school, the administration didn't do anything about getting him to stop bullying other children. They just let it go. As a result, my mother thought it would be better for her daughter's security and safety, if she changed my school.

There were also some noticeable differences at the private school - we had to wear uniforms and it wasn't as close to my house as the other school. The distance from home to the new school required that I either take the train or the bus. If I took the bus it was about a 20 minute ride. At this school, I was also one of the few Black Americans. Let me explain what I mean by that. Most of the children that attended this school, had roots from the Caribbean . . . and they immigrated to the States, so as a result, most of them had an accent when they spoke.

My first year at the private school, everything was new for me! The students, teachers, the school, how they taught, even the neighborhood where the school was located was new. I soon found out there were also a few other differences between me and a majority of the students there. I was an American Black going to school in a majority Caribbean community – I didn't have an accent, so it was easy to identify that I wasn't from that community and not having one, made me stand out more in this new community and at times that could make you a target. Eventually, I picked up an accent in order to fit in and avoid this altogether (a survival tactic).

See there is an unspoken tension that exists between African Americans and other Black communities from places like Africa and the Caribbean.

As an eight year old, I had no clue about this but would find out as the years went past, while attending that school. Why does this tension exist? So many reasons why and one of them being that when other communities of African descent come to the United States, they have been told that African Americans complain a lot, they are lazy, don't work hard, they steal and it falls directly into the stereotype that America has for the African American community. A stereotype that has been around for hundreds of years, since the times of slavery, in order to help justify the wickedness of enslaving a group of people based on the color of their skin.

As a result, when Caribbean and African communities come to the States, and are able to climb the ladder of success, moving past Black Americans on this ladder, some of them start to believe these stereotypes or may already have it in their head space before they even came here. They do not realize the institutions such as the media, education, and medical fields, keep these type of lies, stereotypes, and controls in place purposely, as they may advance in the community.

In addition to that, you also have some people who do not like themselves based on the color of their skin in the Black community throughout the world. An example of that could be that as a darker skinned Black woman, I may not like my darker complexion based on what I have heard in society about myself, I may have not seen enough of a reflection of myself in the media and when I do see myself, it is in a negative light. What I have seen is that darker skinned women are portrayed as not as beautiful and lighter skinned women are placed at the forefront as what being beautiful is.

That means the closer you are to white the better – that means the lighter the skin, the more European features (the smaller nose and thinner lips), the longer hair with soft curls, and even down to the slimmer body build. Black folks having a hatred of their skin color and it tying into how they treat other Black people, is directly connected to Internalized Racism and plays out as Internalized Oppression.

It has been defined as follows:

"*Internalized racism* has been the primary means by which we (Black people) have been forced to perpetuate and "agree" to our own oppression. It has been a major factor preventing us, as black people, from realizing and putting into action the tremendous intelligence and power which in reality we possess. On a personal level it has been a major ingredient in the distressful and unworkable relationships which we so often have with each other."

"*Internalized oppression* is this turning upon ourselves, upon our families, and upon our own people the distress patterns that result from the racism and oppression of the majority society... The result has been that these distress patterns, created by oppression and racism from the outside, have been played out in the only two places it has seemed "safe" to do so. First, upon members of our own group - particularly upon those over whom we have some degree of power or control, our children. Second, upon ourselves through all manner of self-invalidation, self-doubt, isolation, fear, feelings of powerlessness, and despair." (taken from article called Internalized Racism A Major Breakthrough Had Been Achieved from Re-evaluation Counseling.

https://www.rc.org/publication/journals/blackreemergenc e/br2/br25sl)

In the history of the Unites States and the institution of slavery, there was a practice on many plantations where lighter skinned Blacks were often placed in the kitchen to work, while darker skinned Black folks were in the field working. White society preferred lighter skinned Blacks and this is an example of what they would do in our society.

So of course the type of work darker-complexed, as opposed to lighter skinned Blacks, were given, was harder. Picking cotton in the heat for hours a day is definitely harder physical labor than being in the kitchen – this delegation based on complexion. Now you are playing one group of people against another, based on their skin color and the type of work they may be tied to.

Though this history is multifaceted, I am painting this picture since it is important to have an understanding of how racism and colorism has occurred and played out in our society. How it has impacted people in our society and how we do things in our culture. Lastly, to see how this internalized racism and oppression from another adult, towards a child, impacted a third grade girl and impacted my life, well into adulthood.

 During my first year at this private school, I had a teacher named Mrs. L who was short in stature, wore glasses, had darker skin, like myself and was pretty strict with her class. For instance, I recall that during math time, she would walk between the student's desks, carrying a ruler while calling out different math problems like, "What is 5x7?" or "What is 8x8?" and call on certain students as she walked between the desks.

She would identify different students to answer the problem and by the time she got to your desk, if you had not answered the multiplication problem correctly, she would hit the back of your hand with the ruler . . . pretty damn hard as I recall. See at my other school, I had not started learning the multiplication table yet so as a result, I got hit a lot on the back of my hand in this class. I would try to count on my fingers in order to figure it out, but she did not allow this and didn't want to see my little fingers counting under my desk. That would get you hit as well!

I think children are intuitive and can tell when an adult likes them . . . and when they do not. Mrs. L did not like me and she also treated me differently from the other children and was just not nice. I remember another time when she was teaching us how to write cursive and she was very harsh about that. When I was first learning cursive, I used to place my paper straight when I was writing and she would come past my desk, turn my paper at an angle and tell me what I was doing was wrong, and that I needed to work harder or do it again. She was at my desk, a lot! As a result, both writing cursive and doing math, were definitely not my favorite topics to learn!

During lunchtime, the lunches they served at school typically had a little container of milk and the applesauce was placed in a little white cup, with each meal. As a child (and as an adult), I did not really drink or care for milk that much, so I never really drank it. I recall one time that when we sat down for lunch, Mrs. L walked past me and stopped where I was sitting and stated that I needed to drink my milk. I replied that, "I don't really like it" and she pressed on how I needed to drink it. Next, she proceeded to open my milk carton, drink from it, then poured the milk in my applesauce, mixed it around, ate from it, and said how good it was and that I needed to try it. I was so grossed out and horrified! I was truly not going to eat that now. I just let it sit there and looked at it, disgusted.

Those were just some of the things I had to deal with having her as my teacher and knowing she did not like me. In addition, Mrs. L used to call me the "Black, fat American girl" (Yes, I was chubby and so was she). So when that is your introduction and how you are known as a child to the teacher, to someone in authority, then you look at yourself differently.

I already knew I was chubby, but being singled out as Black, even though all the other students in my class and at the school were also Black, made me feel like there was something wrong with my Blackness, with my dark skin. And the way she said and emphasized the word Black, like it was a shameful thing, like it was ugly, made me not like the color of my skin, the darkness of my skin. I thought, "Maybe I would not be called that if I was lighter skinned, maybe she would treat me better.

This expressed colorism by my third grade teacher resulted in me internalizing a strategic desire for boys with a lighter skin complexion. My belief behind that was if I had children one day with that person (I am not sure why this is what many teenage girls think of first), I didn't want them to have a darker skin complexion like myself, so it was better for me to like a boy that was lighter.

When I entered my senior year in high school, I actually really started having a crush on one of my classmates, who had darker skin like myself and I was just like, "I can't believe that I like him!" He was darker skinned like myself and I was confused on why I found him to be so cute? As I reflect on this, it is sad and shameful that I would feel this way.

Beauty comes in all skin colors and this shows how I was not liking myself, nor seeing the beauty in myself.

When I was in my twenties, I started working on shifting my attitude about my darker skin. I was trying to figure out exactly when this may have begun, but I don't exactly recall, but maybe there were a few reasons why.

I do know one thing that had an impact on me were the gorgeous, strong, brilliant, influential, dark skinned Black women in my life at that time. I attended Evergreen State College - Tacoma campus that was founded by Dr. Maxine Mimms, who started this campus in her kitchen, and Dr. Joye Hardiman, who was the director of the Tacoma campus, which I attended for two years. Both women were royalty! They have a deep, rich dark brown skin complexion, and were absolutely brilliant in their philosophy and thought processes. I took dance class with Makeda Ebube, who is also a beautiful, dark skinned woman, that makes dance look effortless. She moves like flowing water and always gave us words of encouragement, as we would be dancing to the beat of live drummers!

I started seeing the beauty in myself so at home, I reflected that beauty with hanging up various pictures of darker skinned Black women and thought, "If I can see the beauty in them, why can't I see it in myself? For myself?" I thought that I needed to let go of what I heard this teacher from third grade say to me, and get past those negative thoughts about my skin complexion.

When I had my son at the age of twenty seven, like many parents, I thought he was the most beautiful baby I had ever laid my eyes on! The love I felt for him was overwhelming! Quentin has a darker skin complexion like me, and I knew that I had to completely pull myself together all the way, for his sake. I didn't want him to grow up not liking his darker skin and doubting how handsome he was. Having my son finally closed the circle of doubt on how I looked upon myself.

I wanted him to have a strong foundation of who he was, to appreciate and love his skin color. I would get him books, dolls and toys that looked like him and the darker they were, the better! I felt that if he had a strong foundation of self-pride, no matter what came his way as he got older, he would hold on strong to who he was as Black child, with darker melanin. I would tell him how pretty his dark skin was, to be proud of whom he was, and where he came from as a Black person. I believe that in teaching him to love himself, I learned to love and appreciate my darker skinned complexion even more!

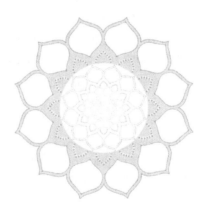

Medicine Stories: A Soul Retrieval Journey

Tomas El Rayess

My inner journey started the day I went straight into the hidden parts of my existence to bring my soul fully home.

What is the function of life? I remember feeling the answer in my soul at an age I couldn't put the question into words. To pass on what has been learned, care and protect one's life and others while joyfully appreciating eternity right here and now.

All children need 3 essential things to develop a thriving body and soul.

They need unconditional love and acceptance from multiple adults, not just mother and father.

Children also need to have the right to just be. They need to not have to make their relationship with their parents work. They don't have to be pretty or compliant, or extraordinary.

And they need the freedom to experience all the positive and negative emotions that nature has blessed them with.

Behind every illness lies a childhood prohibition to do something you desire, a command to do something you do not wish to do, or a sheer absence of either.

The childhood fear of not being loved or abandoned triggers soul loss. When the child keeps changing their authentic self to receive their parent's love, their intimate beauty turns into illness.

Health is only found in authenticity. There is no beauty without it. And to arrive at what we truly are, we must also eliminate from our body what we are not.

Tomás El Rayess specializes in helping you grow a strong gut and self through soul work, authenticity, and the delicious medicine that is food.

He has traveled the world from a young age and collected knowledge, experience and recipes which he turned into a system integrating ancestral nourishing traditions and science. His gut health work focuses on the 9 main food groups to restore your gut health and metabolism. www.tomasrayes.com

Tomás grew up differently than most people. Surviving trauma made him seek tools to make sense of his body, soul, and place in the world. He has created a system to bring your soul fully home to your body, refine your values, needs, desires, beliefs and personal practice for an intentional life.

He is the founder of a health food company, Fuego Ancestral, and his retreats and workshops offer experiences and tools to cultivate the act of creating a good life. www.fuegoancestral.co

Steph's very compassionate and super insightful, not at all complacent. She's very demanding but provides so much value and opens up your mind in a way that you didn't know you could. You see things under a new light, from a different perspective. This is done through very specific exercises that seem almost effortless - they ignite so much creativity and insight. The whole experience is life changing! ~ Tomas

"The Shamans say that being a medicine man begins by falling into the power of the demons. The one who pulls out of the dark place becomes the medicine man, and the one who stays in it is the sick person. You can take every psychological illness as an initiation. Even the worst things you fall into are an effort of initiation, for you are in something which belongs to you."

~Joan Halifax

"The Creator gathered all of Creation and said,

"I want to hide something from humans until they are ready for it. It is the realization that they create their own reality."

The eagle said, " Give it to me. I will take it to the moon."

The Creator said, "No. One day they will go there and find it."

The salmon said, " I will bury it at the bottom of the sea."

The Creator said, "No. They will go there too."

The buffalo said, "I will bury it on the Great Plains."

The Creator said, "They will cut into the skin of the earth and find it even there."

Grandmother mole, who lives in the breast of Mother Earth, and who has no physical eyes but sees with spiritual eyes, said,

"Put it inside them."

And the Creator said, "It is done."

~Hopi Creation Story

FOREWORD

How do you first come back to your body and your existence fully? And then, how do you recognize this person? What do they do? How do they live? And how does this person relate to others? What do they value?

In August 2023 I hit an important milestone in my journey to bring pieces of my soul back into my body. In this quest, I also removed parts that didn't belong to me from my existence. Parts of my family of origin that I had internalized, or parts of my wounded inner child who grew up in neglect, chaos, and abandonment. I realized I had stripped my blood, beliefs, and body of what didn't belong in it. Stories, conditioning thoughts, and behaviors that belonged to others: father, mother, siblings, ancestors.

I realized I had structured my blood with my intention, much like you structure water. This realization felt like the joy of harvesting the fruits of 4 years of deep inner journeying.

I tracked, I retrieved, and I claimed my existence as I got hold of what belongs to me.

I sustained my attention and my practice, peeled layers of family trauma, and dared to look within into my darkest places. I learned to put myself first, I allowed myself to feel the pain and anger, and, like a ruthless editor... started trimming what was not aligned to my own personal values, needs, and desires.

I learned to embody my existence and do everything with love, not for love.

In the process of identifying the values I hold most sacred, I realized these values were not collective, but my own.

Anything that didn't feel loving, peaceful, wise, luminous, filled with gratitude, with vitality, and abundant, I removed from my actions and my thoughts.

I realized all the negative experiences in my life were triggers to jumpstart my gifts, and my response-ability to own my existence.

I learned to acknowledge I am a childhood trauma survivor.

I learned I had internalized other people's realities into my sense of self.

I learned I could ask for help.

I learned I was powerful.

I learned I was imperfect and that feeling all of it was ok.

I learned I could rewrite my complete reality.

I learned that the only opinion of me that matters is my own.

I also learned there are a handful of people I feel safe with and I can call my soul family.

I learned that illusions are real and I had projected my own onto people too close to me.

I learned to let people be who they are, and allowed myself to see them as such.

I became the owner of my existence and the steward of my life, in this body.

I learned to make powerful choices.

Most importantly, I learned I was worth being.

My existence started feeling safe. I learned I could love myself.

For the first time in my life I felt I was fully home.

Here are some medicine stories for you.

My first memory. 1979.
How can this world hurt so much
and be so delicious all at once?

I was sitting at a table on the beach with my father in the Colombian Pacific coast. He had left my mother when I was 1. My mother had just left for Paris and I had just turned 3. There was a cooking fire on the beach and the aroma of flames, smoke, and ocean breeze was perfect in my little soul. The table was set with wooden mallets and I was eagerly waiting for the server to bring the freshly boiled blue crabs.

The Legend of Time. My family beyond spacetime.
July 2020.

I had watched a Spanish series called The Ministry of Time the night before. The ministry of time was a team of people who traveled through portals into the past to make sure that no one changed the course of History.

In the episode I watched, one of them brought Federico Garcia Lorca to 1979 Madrid. They went to a bar where Camaron de La Isla was singing The Legend of Time, a poem composed by Lorca back in 1933. When Lorca heard him singing, he smiled and said:

"That's my poem... so much time has passed and they still remember me... I have won! I have won! Not them.. [Franco and the dictatorship]... Well let's not change a thing then." he said, knowing that he'd be killed a few years later in the 1930's.

I had goosebumps all over my body. I wasn't sure why, but my body felt the electrifying signature of some truth. I was moved, turned off the TV and went to sleep.

The following morning I was enjoying some coffee and the morning sunlight in my ground floor apartment's front yard, looking at the massive green wall across the canyon. It was early, you could hear the birds, parrots, and macaw couples that flew by. You could hear the river far down below.

I thought, oh... let me play that song again. I pressed play on Spotify, started listening while I looked up at the gorgeous sky. The blue was crisp, the clouds fluffy, and I started crying like a lost little boy. It wasn't easy for me to cry back then, and I was bawling.

As I looked up at the sky, I felt this profound nostalgia for my family from elsewhere. "I miss you so much" I thought..."will I ever see you again?" my family beyond spacetime... I played the song again that afternoon and cried one more time, tears down my cheeks, longing to reunite with my family that I hadn't seen in this lifetime.

Your Place in The World.
Nov 2022. Bogotá, Colombia.

One weekend, deep in medicine, I met my family from elsewhere, clearly not from Earth.

I was standing in front of a theater stage where I could see my astral family silhouettes behind a stained glass. They were about twice as tall as regular human beings. We communicated telepathically, and I asked if we could talk. They replied in thought: We are always here for you, and you can communicate with us mentally. The only clear messages coming from them were internal states: feelings of love, light, and a deep sense of calm or inner peace. It felt soothing, safe, and relaxing.

I also met my grandparents on both sides of the family.

First my paternal grandparents, a Lebanese couple who migrated to Colombia in the early 1900's. I was in a living room with them, and asked if they wanted to talk. They weren't even aware I was there with them.

Next frame, I was in my maternal grandparents bedroom. I used to see them only two weeks a year, when my parents would fly me to Colombia from Paris for the summer holidays. I asked them if they wanted to talk. They weren't aware I was there either. I approached my grandmother and poked her in the shoulder. She fell sideways. I was startled, realizing she was a mannequin. Not a person.

Instantly, I was in front of an endless line of ancestors. I could see images of raids, wars, blood, pillaging, cries, battles. There were forest fires in the background. Scenes from a distant time. Until one of them said:" Heeeelp..." and I replied "no, we're doing the work here for me, you have already lived".

As I said that, I was in a place beyond spacetime with my younger self, he was about 8 or 9 years old. He was holding a present in his hands, his smile was mesmerizing and radiant. He looked so happy and grateful.

The present said: My Place.

His smile was saying: "Thank you for doing the work for both of us.

Thank you for giving me my place in this world."

Totem Animals. The underworld. The Ice Age Tribe. Paris-Bogota 2023.

We took nothing. We were on Skype. Sheyma said she would play some drums on her phone. I closed my eyes and asked my totem animals to introduce themselves, as instructed. She reminded me that even though I may interpret visions as my own imagination, or visual stories I would be telling myself, they would actually be shamanic journey visions. I felt some resistance as I eased into the experience. Breathing deeply and slowly I finally ran into a crow and an owl. They guided me down what clearly looked like a European forest path to a clearing. There was a druid tending to a cauldron over a fire. He looked powerful and lonely. Then a shaman deep in the Amazon jungle around the Apaporis river. He looked powerful and lonely too, as if asking to be left alone.

We went for a second round. Sheyma instructed me to ask my totem animals to take me to my underworld. My crow and owl guides took me straight into a house. The basement and the attic were the "world of the below" where things were hidden, and where I had to go to search for parts of me I didn't even know I had misplaced. The visions showed me my underworld was actually Colombia. This tropical country, chock full of hundreds of tropical fruits, majestic nature, great smiles, sensuality, and warmth, also fraught with trauma, abandonment, violence, scarcity, disparity, and hatred, where I was born and quickly taken out of. That was my shadow place, where I had repeatedly come back to gather pieces of my soul.

And a third time we went. This time she instructed me to ask my totem animals to take me to the moment I may have developed the belief that in order to be my shamanic Self I had to be alone again. I was shivering. I was standing on a vast ice landscape, a sabertooth next to me and a fairy, the size of my palm, floating about with us. I had a sense I'd been separated from my tribe, and just the three of us were left. Had they all been killed, had we got lost? I don't know, but it was just the three of us. Me, and other beings who weren't human. Smilodon, ancestor of all big cats or not, representing my ordinary world and connection to the Earth. The fairy, the spirit of nature and the forest. I wondered as I looked afar, whether I could sense the birth of a new collective agreement of isolation for humanity. No more tribes, only couples fighting for their life and offspring on their own? I reminisced about how happy I was when I lived in community in Santa Monica.

Out of here. Beyond Food. The Thomas Fire. 2016 – 2017.

We started 2017 with an ectopic pregnancy, outside of the womb. Our only options were surgery or chemo. We went in for surgery. The danger and stress brought us back together, if only for a little while. Our relationship was already broken beyond repair.

Around spring that year I was making lunch at home in Topanga, and my partner and her 4 year old daughter were having one of their regular shouting bouts.

I was done. I had finally realized how little I loved myself then and how I had stayed for almost 4 years with a woman who had a baby that wasn't mine, who didn't want to have children with me, and I was raising another man's daughter while being constantly reminded I wasn't papa.

In a moment of painful realization, I thought: "I'm out of here". The little girl turned around and said: "Yes, you're outta here". The three of us froze for a long second, and my girlfriend said: "What?" I acted like I had no idea what was going on as I processed the fact that the little girl had read my mind.

The beginning of the end was actually the day we moved into the Topanga house in June 2016.

She was away for work at a women's retreat so I was on move duty. The movers got to our new home, brought everything in, and as they were leaving, I saw a large column of smoke behind the nearest hill. Immediate evacuation for all of Topanga residents until further notice. I ran into the house, grabbed our passports, cash, and my laptop. I was only allowed to go back 6 days later.

That was my first fire.

We only got to enjoy the house for about 3 weeks because I had planned a big summer holiday. I was turning 40 in August 2016. We went to Poland, Morocco, Paris, and Croatia for about a month and a half. It was fun, sweet, gorgeous, as were all of our trips and time in nature. Our daily life on the other hand, now that was a disaster.

Fast forward to July 2017.

They would both usually leave for Warsaw in July. We decided we were going to separate. I was also launching my documentary worldwide. For my birthday that year, I packed my car with personal stuff and my library, and left everything else behind: Kitchen stuff, Moroccan rugs, memories, pieces of me, and a relationship that had been broken for far too long.

I moved back to Venice Beach where a friend had a spare bedroom. To add insult to injury, 4 of my regular clients left town for different reasons. They went to the Hamptons, Maui, etc. I felt my life was imploding, wondering whether I was being punished for something and why my world was burning.

I also thought that people knew me for my work in LA, I would get new clients, it would be alright. One day, one of the top nutritionists in town called me and asked whether I was used to billionaire houses and working with them. She had a potential client, a family in Beverly Park. Their teenage daughters all suffered from gut issues. I met with them, and we decided to start a trial week the following Monday.

That morning, the client called me and said: "We've been evacuated, there's a fire nearby. I'll call you once we're back." I saw the news later that day. They had been evacuated because of The Thomas Fire. Right. I got it. That was my cue from the universe to leave my previous, ordinary world behind.

5 months later I embarked on a one and a half year journey around the world. I had no clue where I was going to land next.

It was the day after a gorgeous 4th of July party in 2019 with friends and DJs on the beach in Venice that I decided I was ready to go back to my Colombian underworld to take care of some pressing blood matters. Family and personal trauma I was no longer ok carrying in my body. I got to Bogota in August 2019.

Last July 2023, while enjoying time with friends in LA and Valle de Guadalupe, I found out that the Thomas Fire had originated in "Los Padres" National Forest. How fitting. Reality truly is a fluid reflection of your inner world.

Tobacco Curandero Medicine
Oct 31st 2019

Have you gone where no one else can go, to retrieve what is yours, and where only you can belong?

The day I met J we were sitting at Delcy's sculpture atelier. He doesn't usually come to Bogota, a friend told me. We sat in the tiny council room adjacent to the atelier on small wooden stools from the Amazon. I sat across from J. This was Delcy's 'mambeadero', a room to sit, have some mambe (ground coca leaf with yarumo ashes) and ambil (a tobacco paste), and share in profound conversations. Ambil tastes exactly like what you may imagine tobacco paste tastes like: bitter, strong, earthy, pithy. We sat there, sharing stories, talking about what we do, and J shared his ambil with us. After a while I noticed he grabbed a bit of ambil with the tip of his index finger and started whispering inaudible words to it. While I wondered what he was doing, I also kept talking to other friends who were there. He pointed his finger at me and said: Here, take this and have it. I grabbed the ambil from his finger, and put it in my mouth. I sat there, taken aback. The tobacco tasted like flowers, fruits, sour, sweet, salty, spicy, bitter. It tasted like everything.

Wait a second, did you just change the ambil flavor with your words? I asked.

He replied: I just showed you what is possible in case you are interested.

I texted him the next day and asked if I could have my own ambil to start my inner study. He had asked me what I was doing in Colombia.

Every night, you'll sit at 9pm and introduce yourself to the tobacco

214

spirit. You will say: tobacco, you were given to us to put order in the world. I, Tomas El Rayess, ask you to come with me to look at what is hidden.

And then what do I do? I asked.

Whatever comes through belongs to you. I cannot tell you what to do. Just the intention. Then it is up to you and your intuition.

That was the day I started a journey into the hidden parts of my existence to track pieces of my soul I had misplaced, and discover beliefs, traumas, stories, conditioned behaviors I wasn't even aware about.

I kept a journal and paid special attention to my conversation with the universe, synchronicities around, and those moments when you feel there is an electromagnetic discharge because something has clicked into your existence, a bond has taken place, charged with pure meaning.

After a month of looking at what was hidden, the next task he gave me was to see what was hidden.

The first time I had seen a tarantula hawk was in Venice in 2014. It was crawling in my backyard. I had never seen a wasp that size, with a shiny metal-blue body and red wings, strolling through the grass. The second time I saw one was around November 2019 in Valle de Cocora in Colombia, next to Salento, about a month after I started my study with tobacco. It was dead and dry, by the stone fountain in the inner courtyard of a country house. Tarantula Hawks lay their eggs inside tarantulas, hence the name. The larvae hatch inside the spider and start eating it from the inside, leaving the vital organs for last, until they are large enough to survive by burrowing out of their host.

That afternoon while on a sunny hike we got to a river and felt like swimming. As I put my bag to the side I hit a wasp nest. I was lucky they were tiny wasps as one stung me in the forehead. Sorry sorry! I said... and walked away as they relaxed.

It was time for me to stop laying eggs in other beings. That part of me had died. It was time to bring my attention back to me. That was the day it dawned on me that I needed to start a reparenting process. It lasted 4 years.

In August 2023, back in Bogota after a few weeks abroad, I felt I couldn't process thoughts clearly or decide on anything. As if my processing and creative power was taken away from me. I wrote to J and asked him for an ambil to bring order back into my mind. He mailed it and sent a voice message that said:

"Oooh. Here is your prayer:

"Father, you who created Man organizing his body with tobacco plants.

With its leaf you made his heart.

With its sap you made his blood.

With its branches you built his arms.

Today, I take my ambil and ask it to rebuild my body

So that all it desires may have a guaranteed and orderly action."

And you blow on it softly, infusing it with your intention."

That was the last month I used these traditional plant medicines from the Colombian Amazon. I thanked them for their company and support as I realized I didn't need them anymore.

It took me a while to fully understand that a long cycle was ending. I had crossed a finish line.

Ancient Fire.
Northern California, 2015–2016.

I went to my first of two ayahuasca ceremonies in 2015. We drank the medicine two nights in a row and both times, I had the same experience: I purged, and purged again, over and over, and saw nothing. Quite the underwhelming experience. Or so I thought.

A couple months later I was asleep at home in Santa Monica. In my dream I went out to the garden in the middle of the night. I was carrying my stepdaughter in my arms as I walked out to the grass, and I saw a black jaguar sitting in the garden path a few meters ahead of us. He stood up and walked towards me on his hind legs, like a man, looking at me straight in the eyes. He approached and handed me a white sage leaf. I woke up sweating, my heart racing, goosebumps all over my body.

After Thanksgiving we rented a house in Joshua Tree. It belonged to a couple of artists. It was beautifully decorated and I felt I needed to go up the stairs to the second floor. As I reached the end of the staircase, there was a large colorful painting right in front of me. The face of a man with a hawk mask. He wasn't wearing it over his eyes but on his forehead. It looked like he had four eyes, his and the hawk's. The painting read: Thomas, hawk boy visionary, soaring fearless.

A few months later I left for the Colombian Amazon with Paul, a British friend. Everything about that trip was wrong. Our guide was stuck in Sweden, then showed up drunk two days later to the speedboat at 7am, and finally sent to jail for corruption we would find out a few months later. I saw anaconda skin patterns everywhere in the jungle. Especially on trees and vines hanging from the canopy.

A few days after having landed back in LA, I sat down one day and drew the logo for Fuego Ancestral, my gut health food brand. The logo depicts the eyes of a jaguar, a hawk soaring fearless, and an anaconda/ouroboros around the whole scene at sunset.

7 years later, I found out that in shamanism, those three animals represent the three main worlds from where the multiverse unfolds: The underworld, the middle world, and the upper world.

The Beginning.
East Village, NY 2012

My deepest desire 11 years ago was to feel healthy in my body and safe in my existence above all else.

My deepest desire 30 years ago was to be anyone else but me.

My deepest desire 5 years ago was to heal my soul. I didn't know I would structure my blood and remove memories and experiences that didn't belong to me. I didn't know I would harmonize the emotions and beliefs installed in my body.

One day in 2012 I could no longer deny I was not well.

I had to acknowledge I was sick in my physical, mental, emotional, energetic, and spiritual bodies.

I had to acknowledge that I needed help, that there were things I did not know. Starting from the negative was the gateway on my journey to healing.

Life put just the right amount of pressure on me to feel such discomfort within that I had no choice but to pause and face this fear.

I was born in Colombia and grew up in Paris without relatives, in a foreign country, without any safe, loving guidance, responsible for myself from age 6.

Father far away physically and emotionally. Narcissistic mother, hypercritical, unregulated, doing heavy drugs at parties, emotionally unavailable. Corn flakes, nesquik, bare minimum parenting. Zero guidance. But fancy restaurants once a week, and museums, loads of museums.

It all felt wrong. I felt out of place. I developed a sense that my existence was incorrect and that I was from another planet.

A third culture kid with no safe masculine or feminine consistent structures to model from, split between cultures, with a heart wrenching nostalgia for a sense of belonging somewhere, feeling stable, plentiful, and ready for Life.

I felt no bond with them. That's where my anger and pain came from. From the pain my inner child had to endure, creating a survival persona, a people pleaser, a savior, escaping from pain and waiting as if placed on hold, for a humane emotional connection, a glimpse of empathy, or a sign of courage and care.

My closest friends were my safe place. In other people's homes there were families, relatives, kindness and attention, regular conversations and laughter.

I didn't realize then, that one of my superpowers had always been the ability to create an enjoyable existence from nothing. Perhaps fueled by hope of better days, or a childhood instinct to stay present and enjoy the richness in the present moment.

But then came growing up.

I wanted to live in accord with my personal truth. And feel at home in my body, in myself.

2012 was the year my inner voice kicked me in the butt out of the mystic closet. I also started seeing repeating numbers everywhere I looked. The clock on the stove in my East Village flat, my watch, someone else's, in a cab, clocks everywhere

I was terrified to embody who I am, and introduce myself to the world..

It was my most paralyzing fear: To be who I am and participate in the world being that person.

I was in physical and existential pain.

When I moved to NY from Tokyo in 2009 I crashed head on against conventional food in America, and against my own ignorance.

Blood sugar high, high visceral fat, chronic stress and inflammation, severe food intolerances and allergies. Especially gluten and lactose. From the perspective of archetypes, I was allergic to Father and Mother.

I was hiding and looking for answers outside myself about my existence and my place in this world.

There is no bliss, health, satisfaction greater than being who you are, and participating in the world from that sacred place. And yet there I was. Terrified and paralyzed.

I had installed a series of survival beliefs in my body. 'If this then that' conditioning mechanisms:

1. I must be either from another planet or I am an expression of the divine and chose to come play the game of existence by starting from a pretty dark level: being born in a family of fucked up psychoanalysts unable to deal with their own sh*t so that I could enjoy myself creating my life from sheer darkness, some meager building blocks and stop the transgenerational curses.

2. I was constantly told I was never good enough, and in order to receive some love I had to do extraordinary things that were still not enough but if I didn't do them I'd never be worthy of

love.

3. Being me hurt so much I wanted to be someone else.

4. Whatever I had to say/share would be boring and people had no time to listen to worthless blabber anyway.

5. If I spoke my truth, my needs, my values, my desires (If I was myself) people wouldn't love me or reject me for being me.

6. I had to tend to everyone's needs except my own because I wasn't worthy of giving myself attention and care.

7. Tending to my existence was so painful that I'd rather escape outwards and elsewhere.

8. I had to do it all on my own because the humans who were supposed to protect and guide me had abandoned me and therefore it was extremely hard to trust others.

9. I had to walk on eggshells out of fear of constant daily critique.

10. Peace and stability were out of reach, something bad was always going to happen and I'd have to run for my life. I was in constant survival mode.

11. I was always looking for a sense of home outside myself: What is the best place for me to live, when and where will I feel Home?

12. If I expressed my feelings and showed vulnerability people wouldn't love me or abandon me because nobody ever cared anyway or simply had no time.

13. I must always come back to my father's place in my hometown because that's where 'family' is, instead of building my own life and asking them to come visit for once.

14. I will only find my teammate / life partner when I am fully healed.

Like I said, my deepest desire 11 years ago was to feel healthy and safe in my existence above all else.

I needed order in my existence. I needed wisdom (knowledge and experience) to heal, and method (practice and rituals) to embody that still formless yet burning vision and desire.

I asked for help, knocked on doors, and had profound conversations with mentors. I produced a documentary on food and health, moved to LA, cooked for celebrities, became a stepdad, lost babies, had an amazing life, made terrible mistakes, engulfed myself in the flames of my existence, and listened to the cues from the universe when it was time for me to journey to my underworld to retrieve my soul.

Today, 2023, after 4 solid years of soul tracking and retrieving, I am home in my existence. I feel safe in my body knowing that my body is Home. And home feels safe, peaceful, stable, kind, loving, harmonious, playful.

At home I am free and safe to be myself, and I feel my blood and my name are safe now too.

Many things have changed in me and how I relate and act in this world. The previous conditioning exercises have transformed into:

1. Whether I am from another planet or chose a crazy existence game setting this time, I am response-able for recognizing what has truly happened in my life, how I have interpreted the events based on what I value most, removing who I am not from my body memory, and making powerful choices about who I am and how I truly want to live out my existence.

2. I am good enough because I am true to myself. I am no longer looking for external validations of any kind. I do what I do with love, not for love. I am lovable just by being me, free from the need to do extraordinary things to get love or prove anything.

3. I find no health or satisfaction greater than participating in my existence being who I am, connecting and bonding with others who choose to live intentionally and consciously.

4. When I have something to say it is none of my business whether others are interested. The need to communicate is mine, and I know I can request others to listen to what I have to say and acknowledge my reality. How they react to it or whether they get it is not my problem.

5. When I speak my truth, my needs, my values, my desires, people feel the frequency of truth in my whole presence. I no longer care whether I make anyone uncomfortable.

6. When I fill my cup first I am fully charged and I end up attracting people I can kindly help or collaborate with. This was impossible for me for many years. When I started practicing putting all my needs first I caught myself several times in disbelief at the possibility of actually thinking about it. It was mind expanding, incredibly hard at times, but I slowly became better at redesigning my actions accordingly.

7. Tending to my existence has been so healing that I don't feel the need to escape from myself. I know that when I allow myself to feel all the feels I may cry or not, but I know I am safe in all my feelings and I am not going to die. When the going gets tough I can sometimes soothe by unplugging, doom-scrolling or binge watching something for a bit or simply doing nothing but meditating, resting, sleeping, going to the sauna for a week and it's ok. Then I come back home.

8. I know it is safe to stay in my zone of genius and I can delegate, ask for help when I need it. It still takes me a while to trust others but now I can communicate what I value and what I need without fearing being abandoned or not loved.

9. Critiques now sound like an opinion I couldn't care less about.

10. Peace and stability were out of reach, something bad was always going to happen and I'd have to run for my life (survival mode). This one has been one of my most profound experiences. I understood the connection between appreciation for my existence, my self-love and worth, and the experience of feeling safe in this body and life. I focused my attention, put myself first, nurtured a home within and started feeling that the peace, stability and safety I felt at home and in my body were feelings worth coming back to everyday.

11. Home is within, and the safe loving home you live in is a reflection of your inner reality.

12. If I expressed my feelings and showed vulnerability people wouldn't love me / abandon me because nobody ever cared anyway or simply had no time. When I express my feelings kindly and honestly in a sacred space I create connection and trust within my relations.

13. I focus on filling my cup first with my values, needs, desires,

and beliefs. As I focus on what drives my actions I activate my powers and I get "my gold".

14. I share with my partner and we keep on healing and doing the work together.

Today? Mmm.. it also takes a lot more to have access to me than it used to. I am no longer driven by people pleasing, perfectionism, or anxious attachment.

"I am grateful to be alive and feel safe in this human body." It took me decades to be able to say these words.

I had to heal my soul so I could love my body. A strong, wise and loving soul in a strong, wise and loving body.

He let them take his name. Or maybe he gave it up. 1920.

My grandfather, Halim Asaad El Rayess was born January 1st, 1900. He moved to Colombia in 1920. His 4 brothers left Lebanon for Montecarlo, Los Angeles, Philadelphia, and Copenhagen. As soon as he landed in Colombia, immigration officers asked how you pronounced that strange last name and changed it to Reyes. Other immigrants didn't allow that to happen. I ignore the trauma burdens he may have carried but he never went back to Lebanon, hid in the yellow pages as H.A. Reyes, and gave away his last name.

I don't know what led him to make that choice, but that's none of my business.

What is my business on the other hand, is my last name. The name of my masculine bloodline.

I started using my real last name around 2018. About a century after my grandfather renounced his. On Nov 8th 2023, I officially retrieved it and updated my ID, driver's license, passport and everything else.

My name is Tomas El Rayess. Don't let anyone take your name from you.

(Bonus) Grandfather Roger. Dec 5th, 2023. Bogotá

"Hier soir j'ai pleuré mes races". (Last night I cried my races).

I had never cried as hard and as much as I did last night. Roger Waters, you are a powerful shaman messenger. I carry Sephardic, Ashkenazi, Lebanese and Syrian blood in my veins. Genetically, according to 23andme, I also carry the memories and emotional, electromagnetic signatures of countless Spanish, Portuguese, Italian, Indigenous american, Chinese, Southeast Asian, Filipino & Austronesian, Ghanaian, Liberian, Sierra Leonan, Senegambian, Guinean, African Hunter Gatherer human lives before me.

Mother, do you think my blood is wrong?
Mother, do you think my life's a waste of time?
Mother, should I hate my neighbor?
Mother, do you think I am a danger?
Mother, can you tell me if my existence is ok?

I stood confused. Both in awe and appalled at the sight of Grandfather Roger Waters, 80 years strong, still standing on stages, still calling all of us to wake up from the slumber, to open our hearts and cry the pain, speak the collective horror and absolute nonsense. Comfortably numb, stone-cold hearts, a sea of chlorinated gazes, the stench of a fading consciousness.

I held my red and white keffiyeh, left arm in the air, as I sobbed for hourly minutes in intense grief for Palestine, for Israel, for Ukraine, for Colombia.

Some deeply repressed ancestral brothers and sisters' memories in my blood, as well as my own, exploded in tears.

Father, can I cry? Is it ok to cry?
Father, do you think it's dangerous?
Father, can I speak my mind?
Father, do you think they'll kill me if I feel?
Father, can I express my emotions?
Father, can I be angry?

My 5 friends started putting their hands on my shoulders, comforting me with their kindness and touch.

As grandpa Roger said: at the bar we can speak to one another, get to know each other, so we can take care of each other.

For an instant, dancing and harmonizing the cosmos in light and darkness, in love and fear, in kindness and hate, in wisdom and ignorance, we were alive, we sang, we cared for one another, and appreciated the passage of Time.

EPILOGUE

"The value of what you possess increases when as many people as possible can benefit from it. Therefore, you only possess what you give." VI of Pentacles.

I was just asking them for one simple thing. To acknowledge their choices and own the consequences of their actions. To acknowledge my feelings and my perception. That's all I was asking for. Not a different life, not a different experience, not a different father or mother. I wasn't blaming them.

I understood you cannot ask an unhealed person to act the way healed people might. It is not a language they are able or willing to speak. That's when I gave up asking them for what they cannot give.

No wonder I was always drawn to the Truth Commission and other systems put in place to bring peace, relief, disarming, release, healing or reconciliation among people who had done terrible things to others or to one another. Just hearing yourself, or your father, mother, sibling, close friend or teammate finally crack open, acknowledge their mistakes, and say sorry for the choices they made, just that. That is all you need for closure and release, really. The signature of truth and response-ability.

No matter what you did or felt, this energy of acknowledging the truth, and feeling its light decompress your whole existence is pure medicine.

That is the releasing power of owning and speaking your truth. Being who you are. Choosing to be who you are. That is the ultimate present you can give yourself. An authentic magician.

The word Magus (magician) means to be able to, or having the ability to create something new, and the word Authentes, acting on one's own authenticity: Creating your own systems of ecstasy.

As you muster the courage to look within and identify your values, needs, desires, bliss, you must also remove what you are not.

To know yourself you must stop being who you think you are. These may be stories, beliefs, desires, values, habits, patterns of behavior that are shaped by stuff from the past or may belong to others (usually mother, father, or ancestral issues from further back) and constant programming from what you got from adults as a child. Your survival persona. The one that you created in order to get some love from the adults in your life, no matter how unhealthy it may have been.

It may be a long journey down the abyss to retrieve parts of your soul you didn't even know you had lost, either because you had misplaced them, or because parts that didn't belong to you had filled the holes left from the pieces you were missing.

There is only one beauty, only one health, one satisfaction and joy, and it is found in the truth of your authentic existence. In reparenting, and loving yourself unconditionally so that you can appreciate how precious and brief your life is going to be.

And once your cup runneth over, well, it's in your nature to help others do the same.

The work you will do to install yourself fully in your body and existence aims to fulfill one goal: to experience eternity here and now, knowing you are dying yet not today, and you get to become the master of your ecstasy so that you can share yourself with everyone else around.

I just want you to know that you can actually build an existence worth living from scratch, even if you were barely given ashes, disorder, and the bare minimum to survive.

Circumstances don't matter. Only internal states matter.

You can call them states of consciousness, states of being, emotional states. You just need to decide which ones you value above all else. It is your life. It is your existence.

Everything you experience as a thought, as a feeling, as a belief, it is all valid. All of it. The scariest, nastiest, gnarliest, best, most exciting, inspiring. All of it. So long as you speak it. Know it is safe to speak your truth. Always.

The transformation of your consciousness happens through your mouth and your whole body, head to toe, in a system that encompasses your blood, heart, brain, gut, cells, words, emotions, in a conversation between your inner world, and outer world.

Your own toroidal field of reality where each of us gets to experience the inward and outward flow of their own life, including experiences, stories, beliefs, emotions, sunlight, water, air, memories, nutrients, joy, laughter, pain, fear, tears, connection, loneliness, hunger, anger, peace...

The center of your toroidal field is your present.
Standing in the axis mundi of your story.
It belongs to you.
Your center of gravity.
No one can experience it
No one can take it from you.
No one can give it to you.
It is up to you to get to it...
It is Home.

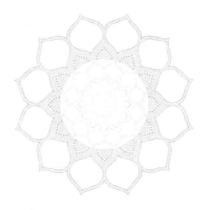

Publishing with Ritz Books

StephRitz.com/publishing

It's time to leave your legacy. What you are inspired to write is meant to be shared - not sit inside of you. Only you can give yourself permission.

Translate pivotal moments of your journey into tangible solutions for your reader.

I love working with others to co-create their dreams... transforming the magic you offer into books, products, programs, and websites.

Explore what it is about you that motivates and inspires others. We'd be a great collaboration fit if...

- You know you have a gift for the world, a vision of changing lives with sustainable and regenerative ideas.
- You see your experiences as life's lessons and know you are a lifelong learner on a journey.
- You challenge yourself to stretch your comfort zone edge.
- And you're committed to turning your dreams into reality.

See how you can take your message to the next level of success! What magic are you desiring to create?

"I've been grateful for and pleased to work with Steph because she's so talented at what she does: the ghostwriting, the publishing, all the how-to stuff... and she also understands what we're talking about. She really has a deep connection to all things spiritual. So when we start raving on about weird things that happened to us, she gets it. And she's able to help us translate that and to say that in a more powerful way. I felt so supported to write this chapter in a book, and to do that successfully! Now I feel confident enough to move on to writing the whole book."

~ Louise Elliott

Collaboration Books

StephRitz.com/collaboration

Come be a part of the next collection of life-altering messages that create legacies, share ancient and ancestral wisdom, open minds, and inspire the future... with stories that change the world!

Together, we'll explore the realm of possibilities. You know they're endless, right?

Ritz Books collaborations are curated to speak out on subjects that society has been known to shroud in silence, with life-altering messages that celebrate individual differences, who we are at the core, and offers glimpses into our shared humanity.

Collaboration books bring together various voices, visions, and values to shed light on a single shared subject.

Included with Each Chapter

11 pages of in a 6x9 Paperback, approx. 3,300 words

- Kindle Edition
- 3 Private 1-hour Sessions with Steph Ritz
- Online Writing Course (Group Zooms)
- Author Speaker Bio @ 150 words max
- Chapter summary @ 250 words max
- Amazon Bestseller Campaign Support

Each author and artist participating in the book project receives structured support throughout the process, and will be a listed author able to link the book to their Amazon Author Page. Additionally, each participant retains all rights to their content.

Steph is an amazing help - my support and edge pusher. I don't know where I'd be without her! She has this way of seeing things that leaves me in awe all the time. She is fun, sweet, serious, EXTREMELY productive, and makes sure that your needs are getting met. ~ Cristina Laskar

---

A Note from the Publisher:

RitzBooks.com

Steph's Sacred Writing Experiences
to Inspire Wisdom from Within

Ritz Books brings together authors and artists from around the world to offer you their healing magic. I hope you enjoyed these life-altering messages that celebrate individual differences, who we are at the core, and offers glimpses into our shared humanity.

It is my wish that these books reveal the potential that lies within your heart, uncover possibilities within yourself, and guide you to embrace ultimately creating individual and global transformation. More than that, I wish to offer you a glimpse into the healing magic you have to offer the world.

What you are inspired to write is meant to be shared - not sit inside of you. Please, don't take what lives inside of you to your grave, don't take tomorrow for granted...

Before departing this life, please share your insights, beliefs, and experiences with the world. Take a moment to listen to the voice of your heart and set your wishes sailing in the sky. It's time to leave your legacy.

What it's Like to Work with Steph Ritz

"For anyone looking to write a book,
Steph is the one to work with."

~ Grace Lawrence

Steph is an incredibly gifted individual who has a true passion for storytelling, and loves working with creatives. I am absolutely blown away at the mastery with which Steph has drawn together collaborative authors from all walks of life to create the powerful Seed series. I am awed at the ease with which Steph was able to hold space for all of us during our virtual meetups, effortlessly sharing her wisdom from her personal experiences and able to ask poignant questions at the right time to help us on our writing journey. I am so grateful to Steph for being to extract ideas out of my head that I didn't know I had. Steph helped me believe in myself as she was able to tune in to me and my written voice in gentle yet powerful ways that truly showcased her experience and love of the written word. I feel that the person I was when I started the collaborative book journey to who I am today are two very different people, and I now feel that I am more confident in my storytelling abilities.

~ Roza Bann

I didn't expect to be taken on such a deep journey of self-exploration, and having a guide on this journey helps to make it richer and fuller, and to enrich my experience and help me to bring my message forward.I'm grateful I found Steph, and I consider her my secret weapon.

~ Julia Lewis

Ritz Books Authors

Adhana McCarthy, Illinois

Agnes Barna, Sydney, Australia

Angela Heart, California

Annie B. Kay, Massachusetts

Banton Dyer, Texas

Cristina Laskar, California

Cynthia "Oya Gbemi" Barnes, Florida

Dara Bayer, Massachusetts

Debbie Howard, Texas & Japan

Etoke "Fuatabong Lekeanju" Atabong, Maryland & Cameroon, Africa

Glenys Brown, Perth, Australia

Grace Lawrence, Oregon

Hasti Fashandi, California

Ilene Cohen, California

Jay Rooke, California

Jenny McFadden, Sydney, Australia

Jermaine "Spirit Buffalo" Reeves, Kentucky

Julia Lewis, Virginia

Kimberly "Omiseun" Early, Washington

LaVerne "Nzinga" Gyant, Illinois

Lee Blackwell, Lake Macquarie, Australia

Lisa "AyoDeji" Allen, Pennsylvania

Lorna Patten, Cammeray, Australia

Louise Elliott, Canberra Australia

Makhosi Yeye Gogo Nana Omari, Maryland

Mariyamah "OloMidara" Hill-Sanna, Ohio & Ghana, Africa

Marshall "OmiTosin" Henderson Jr., Tennessee

Mesfen Manna, Kentucky

Michelle Bee, California

Nashid "Koleoso" Fakhrid-Deen (1949-2020)

Nicole DeAvilla, California

Pat Southern-Pearce, Manchester, United Kingdom

Phyllis Douglass (Vox Angelus), California

Preeti Gupta, Kentucky & New Delhi, India

Radcliffe Johnson, California

Ralph Stevenson, Pennsylvania

Regina "Abegunde" Harris, Kentucky

Robin "Osunnike" Scott-Manna, Kentucky

Robin Daw, California

Roza Bann, Sydney, Australia

Sebastian Laskar, California

Sorcha Fraser-Swatton, Mudgee, Australia

Steph Ritz, California

Tomas Reyes, California & Columbia, South America

Vivian Geffen, Arizona

When tested, we are all stronger than we imagined, smarter than we give ourselves credit for, and have the resiliency of a dandelion... for when the light calls, we will rise again.

~ Steph Ritz

Made in United States
North Haven, CT
17 May 2024

52622356R00128